THE MARRIAGE OF HEAVEN AND EARTH

Gregory Szanto practised for several years as a barrister and then a solicitor before becoming involved in Astrology. He resumed his studies at the Faculty of Astrological Studies where he obtained his diploma. He has since served on its Council and is now a tutor at the Faculty. He is also a full-time consultant astrologer, and is married with two children.

The Marriage of Heaven and Earth
The Philosophy of Astrology

GREGORY SZANTO

LONDON, BOSTON, MELBOURNE AND HENLEY

*First published in 1985
by ARKANA, an imprint of Routledge & Kegan Paul plc*

14 Leicester Square, London WC2H 7PH, England

9 Park Street, Boston, Mass. 02108, USA

*464 St Kilda Road, Melbourne,
Victoria 3004, Australia and*

*Broadway House, Newtown Road,
Henley on Thames, Oxon RG9 1EN, England*

*Set in Sabon, 10 on 11 pt
by Columns of Reading
and printed in Great Britain
by The Guernsey Press Co. Ltd,
Guernsey, Channel Islands.*

© Gregory Szanto 1985

*No part of this book may be reproduced in
any form without permission from the publisher,
except for the quotation of brief passages
in criticism*

Library of Congress Cataloging in Publication Data

*Szanto, Gregory, 1944-
The marriage of heaven and earth.
Includes bibliographical.
Bibliography: p.
Includes index.
1. Astrology. I. Title.
BF1708.1.S95 1985 133.5 85-1251
ISBN 1-85063-021-6 (U.S. : pbk.)*

British Library CIP data also available

ISBN 1-85063-021-6

I dedicate this book to
all who love Astrology,
and especially to Clare, Dominic and Samantha

Contents

Acknowledgments — x

1 **What is truth? – A search for meaning** — 1
  1 *A philosophy for Astrology* — 2
  2 *The astrological connection* — 3
  3 *The historical basis of Astrology* — 6
  4 *A philosophy for the Aquarian Age* — 9
  5 *Unity and division* — 12

2 **The nature of physical reality** — 15
  1 *The world of classical physics* — 18
  2 *Einstein's leap in the dark* — 20
  3 *The quantum revolution and the fall of parity* — 23
  4 *The magical universe – the void* — 27

3 **Heaven and Earth – the world of the magician** — 34
  1 *The spiritual world* — 35
  2 *The model of the magician – the Kabbalah* — 39
  3 *Mind – the missing link* — 45
  4 *The symbolic union – the astrologer as magician* — 48

4 **The mystery of time** — 54
  1 *Time in the physical world* — 55
  2 *The symbolism of time* — 59
  3 *Time's wheel* — 64
  4 *The right time* — 69
  5 *The union of time* — 75

5 **A view of the future – prediction and free will** — 80
  1 *The seeds of time – freedom in the physical world* — 81
  2 *Freedom and time* — 84
  3 *Daemonic, chthonic powers – the meaning of freedom* — 89

4	*Each in his prison – the will to be free*	95
5	*The fruit of the vine – fate and free will in Astrology*	101

6	The firmament – reality and perception	107
1	*This life's five windows – duality, the way we see*	109
2	*Objective and subjective universe*	111
3	*A heap of broken images – symbols and models*	113
4	*Shape without form – what we see in the Horoscope*	115

7	Jacob's ladder	118
1	*The union of conscious and unconscious*	119
2	*The union of man – psychology, the healing process*	123
3	*Finding the Self in the Horoscope*	129

8	The fifth dimension	135
1	*What is the fifth dimension?*	135
2	*The world's almighty mind*	139
3	*The wings of the morning – 5D Astrology*	148

9	Number – the pattern behind reality	154
1	*The pillars of the temple – manifestation and change*	155
2	*The dual role of number*	158
3	*The number of the stars – number in Astrology*	162

10	The union of Heaven and Earth	170
1	*The Centre of the Circle – the correlation between inner and outer*	170
2	*God's mirror – A myth for modern man*	175

Notes	183
Index	189

Illustrations and table

Figure 1.1	Horoscope for 7.18 a.m. 15 July 1944	4
Figure 2.1	Horoscope for 7.57 a.m. 26 July 1875	16
Figure 3.1	The four levels of existence	37
Figure 3.2	The Tree of Life with the sephiroth and the major arcana of the Tarot on the paths	43
Figure 4.1	The Sun's annual path through space and time as seen from the Earth	56
Figure 4.2	The correlation of the tides of the year and the day	73
Figure 8.1	A two-dimensional creature will see the two shaded areas as separate	138
Figure 8.2	The five Chakras on the Tree of Life	140
Figure 9.1	Correspondence between numbers and the planetary orbits	163
Table 9.1	The seven degrees of initiation and their correlation with the planets and numbers	168

Acknowledgments

Acknowledgment is gratefully made to Faber & Faber Ltd and Harcourt Brace Jovanovich, Inc. who have kindly given permission to quote from T.S. Eliot's *Collected Poems 1909-1962*.

My thanks are also due to my wife without whose love, patience and support this book would not have been written; and to my two children who have been an inspiration for the future.

Gregory Szanto

Let every soul be subject unto the higher powers. For there is no power but of God: the powers that be are ordained of God. Whosoever therefore resisteth the power, resisteth the ordinance of God.

Romans 13. 1-2

Since in this way man comes to resemble heaven and earth, he is not in conflict with them. His wisdom embraces all things, and his tao brings order into the whole world; therefore he does not err.

I Ching

CHAPTER 1
What is truth? –
A search for meaning

> 'What is truth?' said jesting Pilate; and would not stay for an answer.
>
> Francis Bacon

The aim of this book is to describe the meaning of Astrology. Although Astrology has been studied and practised by some of the greatest minds since the dawn of civilization, there has been no coherent attempt to formulate its fundamental principles. The basic premise of Astrology, that the heavenly bodies correlate with events on earth, is recognized. But why and how that correlation exists remains a mystery.

We live in a divided world. A world which we can only perceive through our senses, and which is separate from us. We have been taught by science that this external world alone constitutes reality. But the world that science has taught us to accept fails to satisfy us. We know that there is another level of reality beyond the material. One that we can experience without being able to explain.

For the mystic, the artist, the poet and the magician, it is the inner world that constitutes reality. The physical world is an illusion. It is something we ourselves create with our minds. On this level there is unity. The external world is but a manifestation of our inner selves which we see reflected in the universe.

Do we then live in a schizophrenic world, divided between the viewpoints of the scientist and the mystic? Certainly there are two ways of looking at the world. But the conclusion that there are therefore two worlds which are mutually exclusive is a fallacy. Both viewpoints are equally valid and equally real. Each represents one aspect of the whole.

Astrology is ideally placed to reconcile both levels of reality, because the world of the astrologer embraces both the physical and the spiritual. What the astrologer does is to look at mundane, physical phenomena and to look for the inner meaning which is symbolized therein. The two levels meet and are united in the moment of time that is the Horoscope.

1 A PHILOSOPHY FOR ASTROLOGY

Astrology is true, but the astrologers cannot find it.

GEORGE HERBERT

The thesis of this book is that Astrology is a symbolic way of understanding reality as a whole. The physical and the spiritual levels, which together constitute the whole, are contained in us, and in the universe of which we are an integral part. But in order to see as a whole, and in order to see the whole in the parts, we need to unite the two levels in us.

This is the proviso, and it places the emphasis initially on the way we see rather than on what we see, for what we see is but a reflection of ourselves. The statement of George Herbert quoted above is correct because although Astrology can provide the union which mankind so desperately needs, in order to provide it, astrologers must themselves learn to see as a whole. Otherwise, they will merely reflect the division that is current in the world around them.

At the present time, astrologers are divided into those who see their subject as a science, and those who believe it to be a sacred art. The former tend to use their rational faculties to analyse what they see, while the latter use their intuition to try to understand the inner meaning. This is perfectly natural and the difficulties involved in combining the two functions should not be underestimated.

What we need to do, in order to see as a whole, is to recognize that the world 'out there' is the same as the world 'in here'. The world that the scientist sees, the world that the magician experiences, the world that the psychologist perceives, is the same world. Each uses his own model to describe what he sees. And each believes that he is seeing a different world.

But it is only the models that differ. The reality behind is the same. We can see a world in a grain of sand. Or we can see only the sand. The astrologer and the astronomer both look at the motions of the planets in the sky. The astrologer sees, or should see, the quality of a moment in time which symbolizes whatever is born at that time; the astronomer sees only the planetary motions.

It is a mistake for the astrologer to model his method on that of the scientist alone, for the task of the scientist is to explain the physical phenomena he perceives. Equally it is a mistake for the astrologer to model himself on the mystic alone, for the mystic is concerned with direct experience. The astrologer seeks the inner meaning which the mystic experiences in the outer form which the scientist perceives. In this way he can combine the two levels which are contained in the same form.

The task of the astrologer is, therefore, to experience, to understand and then to explain. The task is as difficult as it is fascinating, for it involves a realization of the nature of the physical world, the spiritual level of existence and an understanding of the human psyche. But it is also a task which contains its own fulfilment, for its goal is the union of mankind with its source.

2 THE ASTROLOGICAL CONNECTION

How then should we look at the Horoscope? Let us begin by looking at the Horoscope illustrated in Figure 1.1. What is it? The astronomer would say that it is a diagram of the planetary positions as seen from the Earth at 7.18 a.m. on 15 July 1944. The astrologer would say that it is a symbolic representation of whatever came into being at that moment in time, whether it was the birth of a child, the launching of a ship or the asking of a question.

From the rational, and mundane, viewpoint, it is a representation of certain planetary positions at a certain time. What then is the connection between these positions and the baby born, the ship launched and the question asked, at that time?

If we are to understand the connection it is necessary at the outset to appreciate the implications of what can be seen in the Horoscope. In this way we can begin to define the issues and to look at the possibilities with some degree of objectivity. Four hypotheses put forward recently by Dr Rudolf Tomaschek state the alternatives with reasonable accuracy.[1]

4 WHAT IS TRUTH? – A SEARCH FOR MEANING

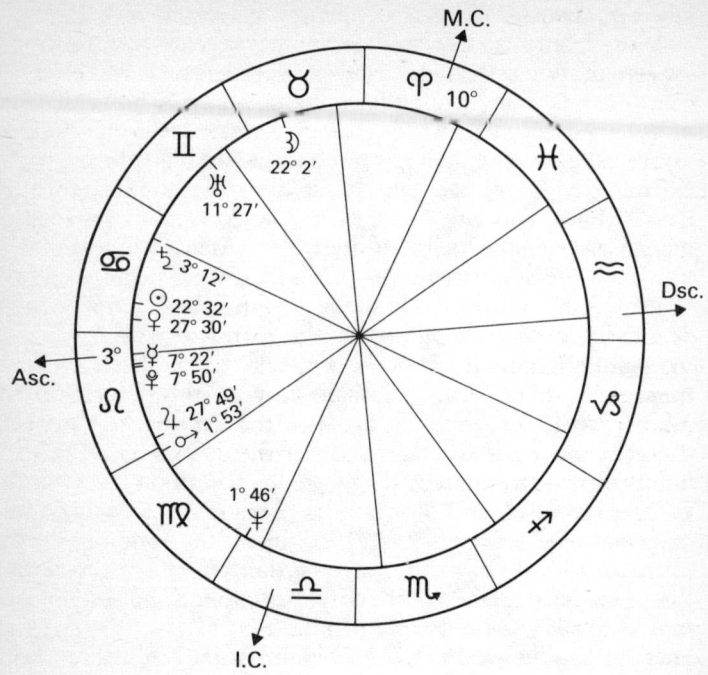

Figure 1.1 *Horoscope for 7.18 a.m. 15 July 1944*

The first hypothesis is that celestial bodies operate on terrestrial events. This means direct causation. The second is that celestial bodies precipitate events which are ripe for manifestation. The third, that celestial events synchronize with terrestrial events. The fourth, that celestial bodies symbolize organic cosmic forces which are qualitative functions of time and space.

Let us take the Horoscope illustrated here as a Birth Chart to see how the implications appear to fit in with these alternatives. First, by looking at the planetary positions, the astrologer can see the psychological characteristics of the newly born baby. He can see, for example, by looking at his Sun in Cancer, that he will be inwardly emotional and sensitive, yet with Leo rising over the horizon, he will project a proud, extrovert self-image.

Second, the astrologer can see the influence of others, his parents and his environment, upon the baby. This child's view of his mother, with his Moon in Taurus square Jupiter and sextile the Sun and Venus, will be stable and optimistic, even to the point of being over-expectant. Now the implication of this is that the relationship between this child and his parents, and indeed the type of relationships he is likely to form in the future, are laid down at the very moment of birth.

Third, by looking at the position of the planets at a later time as they relate to this Horoscope, the astrologer can see the kind of events that are likely to occur in the future. What is actually happening here? The astrologer says that the position of a planet which occupies the area in the sky which contained a planet, or other sensitive factor, at the time of birth, will have an effect on that person.

The Sun in Figure 1.1 was in the area of the sky known as 22 degrees Cancer. When Jupiter occupied the same degree on 5 September 1954, it would have had an effect on the owner of that Horoscope, even though the Sun itself had long since moved away from that point. Indeed, what the astrologer says goes further than this. If a planet is in an area of the sky which is a specified distance from the place occupied by a planet at the time of birth, it will have an effect on that person's life. So when Pluto occupied 22 degrees Libra on 5 November 1980, it would have corresponded with a fundamental change in his life.

If we now take this Horoscope as the answer to a question asked at a given time, in other words as an example of Horary Astrology, the implications are even more profound. Here the answer is quite literally contained in the question. Of course this is also a nice way of illustrating the importance of looking at the Horoscope in the right way.

We can see any Horoscope as an example of Horary Astrology. Instead of looking at a Birth Chart and asking how the individual can use the characteristics that he has been given, we can, in looking at it as a question, ask why he was born at that particular moment in time, and what is it that life seeks from him.

The more deeply we look at the implications, the clearer it will be that there is no simple answer to the correlation. What we should guard against is the temptation to base our conclusions on vague analogies, and this, unfortunately, is what many astrologers have done in looking to direct causation as a possible solution. They point to the physical effect of the Sun and Moon on the tides and the radiation that is bombarding the Earth from the Sun.

No attempt is made to explain how Mercury's position at a certain area of the ecliptic can have a direct effect on a person's mental powers, yet alone how the fact that the Moon is a certain distance from Jupiter at the time of his birth can affect his attitude towards his mother, or how the arrival of a planet at the place where his Sun was ten years in the past can have any bearing on his life.

Direct causation may be an answer. Synchronicity may be an answer. Reality may only be symbolic. It is perfectly valid to state the alternatives. Not surprisingly the hypotheses pose more questions than they answer. In order to try to find the answers we need to probe into the meaning of physical reality and the nature of time and space. And at the outset we need to bear the alternatives in mind so that our approach is open and impartial.

3 THE HISTORICAL BASIS OF ASTROLOGY

> A people without history
> Is not redeemed from time, for history is a pattern
> Of timeless moments.
>
> T.S. Eliot, 'Little Gidding'

When Jung visited the Pueblo Indians of New Mexico he found that they performed a religious rite to help the Sun rise each day. One Indian told him:

> We are a people who live on the roof of the world; we are the sons of Father Sun, and with our religion we daily help our father to go across the sky. We do this not only for ourselves, but for the whole world. If we were to cease

practising our religion, in ten years the sun would no longer rise. Then it would be night for ever.[2]

Let us go back to see what early man was trying to do when he began to formulate the first principles of Astrology. Ancient man accepted himself as an integral part of nature. There was no difference between the external world and his own internal world. Therefore the one inevitably reflected the other.

It was not a question of something in the outside world making something happen. There was only one world. The old saying 'As above, so below' did not mean that what happens in the outside world affects, in a causative manner, what occurs in the world inside. It simply meant that one could see the quality of the time in nature as a whole by looking at external phenomena because outer and inner were identical.

Uranus contacting Mars did not make an accident happen. It was simply an outward manifestation of what was happening in the universe as a whole at that time. Originally our ancestors looked at everything that happened in nature to see the pattern of the moment. When the Babylonians first practised their art, they looked at the planets in the same way as they looked at the rest of nature. Their aim was to be in touch with the time. They knew that the meaning of a particular moment of time could be understood by being open to whatever happened around them.

In Mesopotamia extispicy, the observation of animal behaviour, was practised. The flight of birds was observed. If ants were fighting, it meant that the enemy was approaching. A question was put to the Sun god and then a lamb was slaughtered and its internal organs were examined. So it was the physical appearance of the planets and other celestial phenomena which was important, just as it was the physical appearance of the animal's liver that was relevant. The ancients looked at comets and the changing colour of the Moon.

What was of concern at this stage, before the Zodiac was conceived, was the relevance of the phenomenon to the person experiencing it. Astrology was subjective. Occurrences in the heavens were only valid if they could be seen from the observer's personal vantage-point. So eclipses were only effective if they could be seen at a particular place at a specific time. Thus we read in one of the old texts: 'During the night

Saturn came near the Moon. Saturn is the "star" of the Sun. This is the solution: it is favourable to the king, because the Sun is the king's star.'

It has been suggested that Astrology as we know it today was a mixture of two separate systems. The original omen techniques of the Babylonians with the rationalized mythology of the Greeks superimposed upon it. However, this is an oversimplified view. It is true that the Greeks developed the rational powers of consciousness to a greater degree than their cultural predecessors. But the Babylonians also had their mythology and the process of rationalization was a gradual one.

The first astrologers looked at the world of which they were a part to find its meaning and to experience its meaning more fully. They sought the spirit in nature. They realized that there were certain basic principles in the universe, and that these principles had their seasons and their tides. They felt intuitively the power of fear, of love, of joy, of anger and they knew that these forces existed both in themselves and in the universe and that their energy fluctuated from time to time.

It was from these principles that the god forms were created. The intuitive realization by the Babylonians and the Egyptians of the archetypal forces was conceptualized by the Greeks and projected onto the heavens. The difference of viewpoint is one of degree. The Babylonians saw the essence of the archetypal principles in the universe, including the planets, around them. The Greeks began the separation of the planetary forces from their own nature which eventually led to the separation between inner and outer.

Thus their mythology became externalized onto the constellations in the shape of the Signs of the Zodiac which embodied the living principles of the gods and onto the Sun, Moon and planets which were originally thought of as the bodies which interpreted the secrets of the gods.

The process of building up the god forms can be seen most clearly in Roman times. Sometimes the principle was recognized but not personalized. Fides, Salus, Spes, for example, were appreciated only as principles. Tellus, the power of the earth, was similarly never personalized but it was taken a stage further. Its cult was carried on by the chief pontiff and the

Vestal Virgins at annual sacrifices in the one temple dedicated to its power.

The final stage was evolved in those principles around which a personalized body of myth was created. Mars represented the principle of assertion, aggressiveness and anger which was present in everyone and from the individual force was built up the general form of the god. This process therefore represented a half-way stage between the primitive and the modern mind. It involved the use of consciousness to externalize the essence of the basic principles in life in the forms of gods and goddesses until the essence itself was lost.

Later men began to use their rational powers to work out a system of correspondences between external phenomena and events that happened to them. So there grew up a careful system of correspondences in which what was above mirrored that which was below. Astrology thereby became a meticulously conceived system for the planetary positions which reflected the quality of the times and which could be plotted in advance.

The danger of separating outer from inner is, of course, that one can lose the meaning of both. The aim of Astrology was to be more aware of what was occurring in nature. Consciousness enables us to see nature objectively but in relying too much upon that faculty we can become cut off from our source. We have the advantage of seeing nature without the benefit of experiencing it.

Now, to use Astrology correctly, we need to return once more to our source, but without sacrificing our conscious faculties in the process. The next stage in our evolution will be a synthesis of conscious and unconscious – a marriage between Heaven and Earth. This is the step that mankind is poised to take. Then hopefully, he will be able to return to his original inner nature in the full light of consciousness.

4 A PHILOSOPHY FOR THE AQUARIAN AGE

No one has yet succeeded in inventing a philosophy at once credible and self-consistent.
BERTRAND RUSSELL

Socrates believed that if a man wanted to be a good shoemaker, he must first understand what a shoe is and what it is meant for. There was no point in choosing the best materials and deciding how to use them, until he had formed a clear-cut idea in his mind of the nature of the shoes he was setting out to make.

Socrates's condition is, up to a point, as true today of the astrologer as it was of the shoemaker in ancient Greece. The astrologer, too, needs to have a clear idea of the function and meaning of his subject. The function of Astrology is to help people to understand themselves and to enable them to realize the meaning of their lives. But the nature of Astrology differs from that of shoemaking in that it includes meaning as well as function. Meaning can only be experienced and therefore it goes beyond the strict import of philosophy in the sense of speculative thought. When we ask what our lives mean, we seek an inner significance which is the role of myth rather than philosophy. And this significance cannot be discovered by rational, or speculative, thought. It can only be realized in a way that can best be called spiritual.

There is no spiritual dimension to the shoemaker's craft, certainly not in the sense that Socrates describes it. Equally there is no spiritual dimension in philosophy as Bertrand Russell conceives it. While philosophy concentrates on the attempt to understand rationally the nature of life or a particular aspect of life, as it is perfectly entitled to do, it should come as no surprise that it has not succeeded in being both credible and self-consistent. For in concentrating only on the rational functions it will have as its object only the material level of reality, a level which in itself does not contain meaning. This is the underlying flaw in the philosophic approach. It tries to find meaning in a way which inevitably excludes meaning because it separates the exterior from the interior.

For Russell, reality is contained only in the material, objective world. Although he conceives that what is 'out there' is influenced by our senses and the way we see the objective world, nevertheless it is that physical world which is the only reality. Truth, according to Russell, consists in whatever corresponds with the objective world. As he wrote in his *Problems of Philosophy*: 'Here we are driven back to CORRESPONDENCE WITH FACT as constituting the nature of truth.'[3]

And this fundamental law, what he called the law of identity, states that whatever is, is. This in turn evolved into his law of contradiction which states that nothing can both be and not be.

To some extent it is unfair to take Bertrand Russell as an example of philosophic thought but he does illustrate the best and the worst extremes of philosophy founded on scientific ideology. Science and religion are, of course, each trying to do different things. The task of science is to explain, while that of religion is to provide something to believe in. The problem arises when either attempts to contain the whole truth. Each can provide a partial, and extremely useful, insight into the whole. But the whole can only be seen if the two are combined. Occasionally the two viewpoints are to some extent combined in one individual. One such person was Teilhard de Chardin who said:

> The time has come to realise that an interpretation of the universe, even a positivist one, remains unsatisfying unless it covers the interior as well as the exterior of things, mind as well as matter. The true physics is that which will, one day, achieve the inclusion of Man in his wholeness in a coherent picture of the world.

I believe that this time is now upon us. Man needs a philosophy which will provide him with meaning. He needs to believe and to understand, both rationally and experientially. Up to this moment in history there could be no confluence of these two needs. Science was unable to explain what mystics intuitively understood. Man became alienated from his source. And mystics, turning their backs on the material world, have not been concerned with scientific explanation.

Now the wheel is about to come full circle. Astrology is uniquely equipped to combine the understanding of the physical and spiritual levels of reality, for Astrology embraces both. Through Astrology mankind can at last learn to see in a new way, a way which is essentially astrological.

Astrology is above all concerned with time. On the face of it, it is surprising that for all the thousands of years that Astrology has been practised, no philosophy of its own has been formulated. This, however, is the time for science and spirit to find a living synthesis, and it is precisely at this time that the philosophy of Astrology can be formulated in uniting both.

We all know that we are now in the process of moving from one Great Age to another. We are at the intersection between the Piscean and Aquarian Ages. The period of change is one of flux and uncertainty, and the world appears to lack direction. But from this confusion we shall discover that we are living in the most exciting and important time since Christ upset the world with his message 2,000 years ago.

We are now on the brink of new discoveries and we are on the edge of a new leap in our evolutionary processes. Each Age needs its own philosophy to mirror its thought processes and ideals. As we enter this new Age, we too need a new philosophy. There is a time for everything. And the time for Astrology's philosophy to be formulated is this time – the time of the dawning of this New Age, for the philosophy of Astrology is also the philosophy of this Age.

5 UNITY AND DIVISION

> This is the land which ye
> Shall divide by lot. And neither division nor unity
> Matters. This is the land. We have our inheritance.
> T.S. ELIOT, 'Ash-Wednesday'

According to a Sumerian myth, there was in the beginning of the world a mountain named Anki. And the mountain was one. Its top was An, Heaven, and its bottom was Ki, Earth. Then Enlil, the son of An and Ki, took a sword and cut the mountain into two. Thus did the world as we know it come into existence. Time was born from eternity, division from unity.

But although the mountain was cut in half, it was still one mountain. The top and the bottom were contained in the whole. Division and unity co-existed. This is our world. It is a world where division is contained in unity. A world of paradox; where what is, is not; and where what is not, is.

We can see the division in the world. Between spirit and matter, conscious and unconscious, explanation and understanding, science and art, yang and yin, men and women. We can also, sometimes, see glimpses of the unity. We can see the world as one, as a whole, when this moment of time becomes for us, eternity.

The aim of Astrology is to see the whole in the parts. The key to understanding Astrology lies in recognizing the underlying unity behind the separate factors in the Horoscope. In realizing that our material world, the world of division, of space and time, is the same as the spiritual world of unity, of oneness and eternity, and in learning to see the one in the other.

The temptation is to relate to only one level of existence. To recognize the reality of the material world, the division that exists in the universe and in ourselves, and to believe, like Bertrand Russell, that this is the only world. Or to take the opposite view and to say that this material world is an illusion and that the only reality lies in the spiritual essence behind the physical form.

The aim of mankind is to re-unite the two. Man's quest, his search for meaning, is to find wholeness. Astrology, symbolizing both levels, has the power to achieve the reconciliation of the opposites, or the marriage of Heaven and Earth.

Robert Browning said that 'truth is within ourselves'. But the truth we see depends to a large extent on the way we see. The answers we get depend on the way we ask the questions. To return to Socrates, the first step towards the acquisition of knowledge is the conviction of ignorance, to clear our minds of all previous assumptions and beliefs. The need to be completely open is an obvious one but nevertheless it needs to be borne constantly in mind.

This is the quality of passive acceptance or 'unknowing' as Meister Eckhard called it. Or in the words of Bertrand Russell:

> The free intellect will see as God might see, without a HERE and NOW, without hopes and fears, without the trammels of customary beliefs and traditional prejudices, calmly, dispassionately, in the sole and exclusive desire for knowledge – knowledge as impersonal, as purely contemplative, as is possible for man to attain.[4]

But as Russell himself clearly showed, these qualities are not enough. We may think we are being open, but unless we have learned to see in the right way, we can never hope to see the truth. Most people are afraid to keep asking questions because they know that if they keep pushing back the door towards the truth, they will reach the stage where there is nothing.

The quest for understanding, symbolized by the major arcana in the Tarot, begins with the Fool. He starts his journey by walking with all his possessions on his back, one foot poised precariously over the abyss, the void. His eyes follow the butterfly, symbol of the psyche or spirit. His number is 0 – nothing, and eternity.

One of our foremost modern astrologers, the late John Addey, has said:

> In the last resort it is ideal philosophy and the vision of spiritual laws which will give a secure foundation to our knowledge of all the outworkings of astrological effects. . . . It is only in the light of universal spiritual laws that the details of astrological science can be perfectly formulated.

The true scientist searches for knowledge wherever it leads. Like the true philosopher he is concerned only with the truth. The truth is before us if we have the courage to look. All too often we do not see the truth, not because it is not there, but because we do not recognize it when it is before our eyes.

The beauty of Astrology is that it helps us to see in a new way. Through the symbolism of Astrology we can combine our rational and intuitive faculties and become more nearly in touch with the wholeness that is contained in both. The means to achieve this unity is in the nature of revelation, an inner awakening through allegory, parable, poetry and paradox as well as through logical, rational explanation and speculative thought. It is not easy to combine the two sides but I believe that the effort will provide its own reward.

> We shall not cease from exploration
> And the end of all our exploring
> Will be to arrive where we started
> And know the place for the first time.
> T.S. ELIOT, 'Little Gidding'

CHAPTER 2
The nature of physical reality

> Human kind cannot bear very much reality.
> T.S. ELIOT, 'Burnt Norton'

The task of the astrologer is to find the connection between Heaven and Earth. The domain of Heaven belongs to the magician and this we shall examine in the next chapter. The physical realm is that of the scientist and we shall begin our search for meaning by looking at the nature of the physical world in this chapter.

What is the meaning of the events that take place on the physical level and what is the physical correlation between the movements of the planets and those events?

Why did the person born at 7.18 a.m. on 15 July 1944 have a serious motor accident in December 1972 when Uranus was at 22 degrees of Libra, 90 degrees from the position occupied by the Sun at the time of his birth? Why do other planetary contacts manifest themselves on a psychological, or spiritual, level? Why did the person whose Horoscope is illustrated in Figure 2.1 suddenly develop a deep and lasting interest in alchemy when Uranus occupied 15 degrees of Taurus in June 1936, the exact position in the sky that contained the Moon at the time of his birth?

In order to answer these questions we need to understand the nature of physical reality. Many of the fundamental tenets both of Astrology and of physical science are now being challenged. For centuries it has been accepted that a person born when the Moon is in Taurus will react in a stolid and sensual way to the world. Roman emperors even had their Moon signs inscribed on their coins. Now, thanks to the statistical research of those like Michel Gauguelin, and the scepticism of those like Geoffrey Dean,[1] doubts have been cast on whether there is any intrinsic significance in the Moon's position in Taurus.

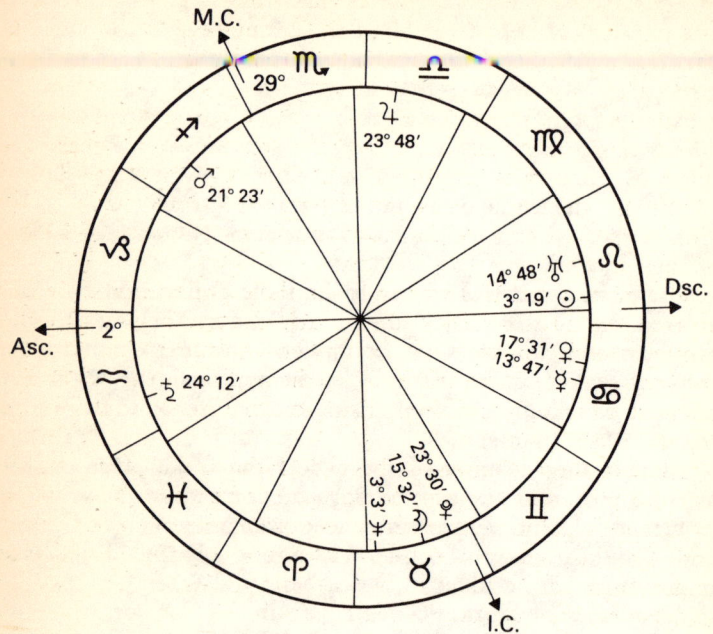

Figure 2.1 *Horoscope for 7.57 a.m. 26 July 1875*

For centuries it had been assumed by scientists that the world 'out there' was separate from those who observed it, and that this objective universe obeyed definite laws. Now, thanks to the discoveries following the quantum revolution and the fall of the conservation of parity, it is no longer possible to assert that there is a world 'out there', yet alone of what it consists.

Both astrologers and scientists have constructed their own models of the world based upon their respective beliefs. Much of the crisis that science faces today is due to the failure to appreciate that the world that has been created in the scientists' image is as much a symbolic model as the Horoscope is for the astrologer.

Now that the old assumptions are proving to be false, now that scientists have found that the basis of the physical world is not physical at all, now that the dividing-line between inner and outer has been broken down, the whole foundation of physical reality needs to be reassessed.

Science views the surface. This is the level of manifestation, where things happen in the material realm alone, where the rules of causation apply. If we take the basic model of Astrology, the circle with the dot in the centre which is the Horoscope, we can see the laws of science, of space and time, of the physical world, in the circle.

The planets travel unceasingly in their predetermined paths around the circumference. The Earth lies in the middle. And around the circumference is the universe – 'out there'. We lie at the centre. And, at the still point in the middle, is the spirit. The scientist sees the circumference alone. The mystic and the poet see the centre alone.

The astrologer combines the two: Heaven and Earth. If the astrologer follows the path of the outer circle, if he bases his art on scientific methodology alone, he loses touch with his centre, and like so many scientific astrologers today, he fails to understand the meaning of his art because he fails to understand the nature of reality.

It is necessary to look at the circumference because it is a part of the whole, and therefore in this chapter we shall see how scientists have viewed the physical world. But scientists have failed to understand the meaning of the physical world just because they assumed that it alone was real. And in doing so they have succeeded in alienating man from nature.

It is quite valid to look for a physical connection between the position of Uranus and a motor accident on Earth; it is perfectly natural to look for causative factors between the two. It is also valid to seek the meaning for this occurrence. The questions that science asks and the questions that Astrology asks are different.

The scientist asks: 'What is the nature of the world out there?' and 'How can I use it?'. The astrologer asks: 'How am I a part of the world?' and 'What is my role in the world?' To answer these questions both need to know the nature of the world in physical terms. The aim, then, is to connect the material sphere with the spiritual centre and to transcend the two by getting behind both.

Science was originally brought in to explain a universe which was intuitively understood by the ancient astrologers. And science has succeeded in helping to explain the working of that universe. But in order to provide the meaning mankind seeks today, science needs to be reunited with the spiritual truths that were inherent in the old astrological understanding of the universe. In the words of the physicist Roger Jones: 'The great lesson that physics needs to relearn from alchemy and astrology is how to put the humane back at the heart of science.'[2]

1 THE WORLD OF CLASSICAL PHYSICS

> There is something fascinating about science. One gets such wholesale returns of conjecture out of such a trifling investment of fact.
>
> MARK TWAIN

Astrology is not an exact science. Nor, for that matter, is science an exact science. Nevertheless, the discoveries of science have been formulated on the assumption that there are definite laws on which the physical world is based. As recently as 1912, Bertrand Russell could write: 'The business of science is to find uniformities, such as the laws of motion and the law of gravitation, to which, so far as our experience extends, there are no exceptions.'[3]

Although it is axiomatic that one finds what one looks for, it can easily be overlooked that the scientists' discovery of uniform, certain laws has been the result both of their own assumptions, and the subsequent selection of that which fulfilled their expectations. In the words of Roger Jones: 'The acid test of any scientific theory is first and foremost, its agreement with the *facts* of the physical world.'[4]

This proposition inevitably assumes that there are objective 'facts' with which scientific theories can agree. But the desire for certainty and for an objective world separated from its observers does not in itself create such a world. In order to appreciate the basis of scientific discovery, it is important to bear in mind the five main assumptions upon which these discoveries have been founded.

First, that there are certain laws which must always be obeyed; second, that the world of matter is objective and that therefore it is separate from those who view it and experiment with it; third, that there is some fundamental building block upon which matter is formed; fourth, that there is a tangible foundation for the world; and fifth, that a thing can only be one thing at a time.

These assumptions can be traced back to the rational and deductive thought processes of the Greeks who performed a useful service in seeking to define abstract principles as a basis for scientific ideas. But the world they created was one which was over-idealized and, of necessity, perfect.

It has been suggested that the Greeks, and those who conformed to their methods, rescued their primitive precursors from superstition and magic. And there is some truth in this admittedly oversimplified view. Magic and superstition were prevalent in the primitive mind and also in those who were followed by the scientists of the so-called Age of Enlightenment. But although their methods were diametrically opposed, both the magicians and the rational scientists were trying to achieve the same goal. Equally both were inspired by a fear of the unknown. The difference was that those who followed the Greeks looked upon nature as something alien; whereas the magicians, although they feared its power, felt it to be a part of themselves. Both tried to control nature. The scientists by creating definite laws which would help them to predict the future. And the magicians by seeking the essence and meaning of the world in which they lived. Whatever they may have thought, each based their conclusions as much on belief as the other.

The aim of science was to find out more about the future by learning from the past. The purpose of the scientists' discoveries of the classical age was summed up by the mathematician Pierre Laplace:

> An intellect which at a given instant knew all the forces acting in nature, and the position of all things of which the world consists — supposing the said intellect were vast

enough to subject these data to analysis – would embrace in the same formula the motions of the greatest bodies in the universe and those of the slightest atoms; nothing would be uncertain for it, and the future, like the past, would be present to its eyes.[5]

With this view of the world as a great machine, it was natural that science should concentrate on acquiring more and more mechanical knowledge about its workings. Inevitably scientists became mechanics rather than philosophers. At the end of the nineteenth century the scientist A.A. Michelson could say that the future of science consisted of: 'adding a few decimal places to results already observed.'[6] That prophetic statement was made in 1894.

There was no freedom or hope in this world. Its relentless logic was inescapable. As Jack Lindsay has written:

> It invented a world of symmetry and reversibility, and imposed it on the real irreversible and assymetrical world, defining stable states alone as real and ignoring everything else – all points of critical change, all aspects of qualitative development. The limits of usefulness in this attitude have now been essentially reached. Hence the general crisis in physics and related fields, which has set in since Einstein, quantum mechanics and the new problems raised by penetration into the particle level. From any general aspect the post-Galilean scientists have been far more blinkered than were the astrologers.[7]

2 EINSTEIN'S LEAP IN THE DARK

Einstein did not accept that scientific discovery was a thing of the past. He was not afraid to take the leap into the dark, to step over the precipice like the Fool in the Tarot, relying on his intuitive beliefs about the nature of the world. Einstein developed the understanding of the nature of matter and of the universe which it composed far beyond its existing boundaries.

Before Einstein shattered the accepted beliefs of his time, matter was accepted as tangible reality. The ultimate building block of the universe had been found. The atom was the basis of physical reality. Rearrange it, play with it, and any kind of matter could be created.

But Einstein destroyed the concept of matter as something tangible. By so doing he opened the way for a completely new concept of physical reality. He was a pioneer in the best sense of the word. But although his mind was great enough to encompass much that his fellow scientists had steadfastly rejected, nonetheless it could not accept the inevitable conclusions of his own beliefs. He could go so far, but no further.

Einstein contributed to the understanding of the nature of matter in two very important ways. First, in his laws of Relativity, and second, in his field theory. But he took neither of these concepts through to their ultimate conclusions. This is not intended as a criticism of a man who on his own widened the scope of understanding to a greater degree than perhaps anyone since Newton. And just as it is unfair to blame Newton for not having gone even further, so it would be churlish to expect Einstein to have gone to the ultimate limits of understanding.

Einstein appreciated that time and space are only relative. That there is, therefore, no universal present and that one man's past could be another man's future. His theory of Special Relativity in 1905 and General Relativity ten years later changed man's whole concept of space and time. Nonetheless he was bound by his concept of the speed of light. He refused to accept that a person or object could communicate instantaneously because they would not be able to exceed the speed of light.

His famous equation $E=mc^2$ meant that matter and energy were convertible. Matter as we normally think of it, is mass. Although it had been appreciated long before Einstein that matter was composed mainly of empty space with the atoms in the molecules occupying only a relatively small area, nevertheless matter as then conceived was something tangible. But with Einstein matter began to disappear completely.

The conclusion that matter is essentially the same as space is inherent in Einstein's propositions. He came to put forward a hypothesis that unified the nature of physical reality into a 'field theory' where each particle produces a rhythmic pattern of energy. As he said: 'We may therefore regard matter as being constituted by the regions of space in which a field is extremely intense.... There is no place in this new kind of physics both for the field and matter, for the field is the only reality.'[8]

In putting forward his unified theory, Einstein was unwittingly treading on very thin ice. He had great insight, he had the vision to see the whole in the parts, he looked up while others looked down. But unfortunately, in looking up he refused to accept what was down there — inside the atom. So while his colleagues were experimenting on the sub-atomic particles, he resolutely shut his eyes to their discoveries.

Although Einstein sought a unified theory of reality and truth, he inevitably failed to find his goal because he refused to accept part of the world and insisted on clinging to his assumptions. One of his blind spots was the quantum theory which revolutionized scientific understanding of matter. Instead of trying to incorporate its discoveries into his own findings, he spent a great deal of energy trying to disprove it, eventually writing it off with the remark: 'God does not play dice.' In so doing he inevitably failed to produce a unified theory which in the words of Bertrand Russell was 'at once complete and self-consistent.'

His other blind spot concerned the speed of light. In his Special Theory of Relativity he proposed that at the speed of light an object would disappear, its mass would become infinite, and time would stop. Or so it would appear to an observer. To the person or object travelling at the speed of light, all would remain as before. Now if one approaches these propositions with an open mind, there are two possible conclusions. One is that it is impossible to travel at the speed of light. The other is that it is possible and that one then disappears, becomes infinite and is outside time. As a logical alternative, either is possible.

Einstein held that the first must be true because the second appeared to be nonsense. I believe that in rejecting the alternative out of hand, he missed the opportunity to resolve one of the great truths of existence. And because his great mind rejected it, other lesser minds followed suit, like those who dared not contradict the views of Aristotle and Ptolemy. The paradoxical nature of light is apparent because although it travels at a finite speed, 186,000 miles a second, yet it interpenetrates the world in an instant. Because of Einstein's blind spot, the nature of light has remained a mystery to this day.

In summing up Einstein's achievements, Nigel Calder wrote: 'Einstein's rule again keeps the universe simple and tidy.'[9] This praise is two-edged. For however great was Einstein's mind and his contribution to the knowledge of the world, he clung to a view of the universe which was based on certainty and where the laws of order and structure ruled supreme. He was the last of the great determinists. He succeeded in adding to the foundations of Newton's world but he refused to believe in the freedom of matter. Mass and energy were convertible, but his equation only emphasized the laws of conservation which Newton had espoused.

Einstein's world was symmetrical, certain and safe. It was the definite, deterministic world of Newton and, like Newton's world, it described the realm of matter at large extremely well. On its own level it succeeded remarkably well for Einstein was one of the most remarkable men of genius that the world has known, as was Newton before him. He inevitably failed to provide the unified theory that he sought because he shrank from accepting the other levels of existence that we shall now examine.

3 THE QUANTUM REVOLUTION AND THE FALL OF PARITY

With Einstein we reached the limit of the determinate world. Upon this structure of certainty, came two revolutionary discoveries. First was the quantum theory. Second was the fall of the conservation of parity. In its own way each of these discoveries dramatically changed man's outlook of the universe and his understanding of the nature of physical reality.

A great deal has been written about quantum theory, understandably enough in view of its ramifications. The philosophic implications are to my mind of even greater importance than any physical effects, and it is vital to see these in the context of reality as a whole if we are fully to understand how and why the universe works. Less has been written about the fall of parity but the implications of that discovery are also of great significance in appreciating the reality of physical existence.

Quantum theory had two important practical effects. First, it was found that at the sub-atomic level change can only occur according to the value of whole numbers. Therefore, at this level nature is discrete and discontinuous. Second, at the sub-atomic level, nature is indeterminate. Its world does not consist of definite laws. On this level the future cannot be predicted from a knowledge of existing forces as Pierre Laplace had postulated. Nor could science be confined to discovering uniform laws to which there were no exceptions, as Bertrand Russell had asserted. The universe had suddenly come to life, it had become a living process, where everything was a part of everything else; where the only reality was change, the still point of a turning world.

Einstein had formulated his famous equation stating that mass and energy were convertible, so that one could be changed into the other. But there was no question so far as he was concerned that they could be both at the same time. And yet this seemed to be the case. At one time an electron behaved like a particle and at another like a wave. How could scientists get round this apparently insoluble problem?

As this dilemma was to divide scientists' views of the physical universe, it is worth looking at in a little detail. The problem itself was highlighted in two ways. First, in the well-known double-slit experiment. In this experiment a beam of electrons are projected through a screen which has two narrow holes just big enough for one electron to go through at a time. The electrons can then be detected when they hit a second screen. In going through the holes individually the electrons act like particles, but when the total number of electrons end up on the second screen a wave pattern can be seen. Therefore, the electrons behave like particles and waves at the same time which, according to accepted scientific laws and, indeed, to common sense, is impossible.

Second, Werner Heisenberg illustrated by his famous Uncertainty Principle in 1927 that one could not measure both the momentum and the position of an electron at the same time and that it was therefore impossible to know if it was a particle or a wave. The point was that in trying to measure the position, the observer needs higher energy light which alters the momentum of the electron, but if lower energy light is used, then one cannot measure the position accurately.

There has been a great deal of controversy about just what this principle does show. Some have held that it simply shows that we cannot measure both, but objectively both do exist simultaneously. Others take the view that the actual attempt to measure affects the state of the electron and, therefore, anything that we look at on this level will be changed by the very act of looking at it. According to Bohr and others, the conclusion that must be drawn is that anything which cannot be measured cannot have reality. Heisenberg himself could not understand how a sub-atomic entity could display the properties of both a particle and a wave. Having talked late into the night with Bohr, he asked: 'Can nature possibly be so absurd as it seemed to us in these atomic experiments?'

Heisenberg's principle has also been termed the principle of Indeterminism because whatever else it showed, it was clear that at the sub-atomic level the determinate structure assumed by physicists did not exist. The objective universe 'out there' was no longer a reality. What is of importance from the philosophic point of view is that because a precise knowledge of present conditions is impossible, so a precise knowledge of future states is also impossible, and thus there is no reason to believe that events on the atomic level are determined in advance.

So what had scientists discovered at the sub-atomic level? They called the 'bits' inside 'elementary particles' and their numbers have proliferated until they exceed even the number of the known elements. Instead of finding the unity and simplicity they sought, they were thrown into even greater confusion and multiplicity. But are these 'bits' real? Are they tangible things that exist or are they only convenient models?

Heisenberg has said: 'In the light of quantum theory... elementary particles are no longer real in the same sense as objects of daily life, trees or stones.'[10] And Henry Stapp has said: 'An elementary particle is not an independently existing, unanalysable entity. It is, in essence, a set of relationships that reach outward to other things.'[11]

Quantum theory has produced a world of paradox. Where phenomena appear to have different properties. Where it is difficult to say that one thing is, or is not. Instead of a world of continuity and flow, particles jump from place to place. Instead of an objective world separate from the observer, the 'out there' ceases to exist independently. Instead of the old order in the universe, it appears that there may be order but order which includes change and diversity in a total concept of reality.

The other important discovery of this century was the fall of parity. When the discovery was made in 1956, the headline 'Weak interaction violates parity conservation' swept the world of physics like wildfire. It was something totally undreamed of and it changed the foundation of the physical world. Until that year it had been assumed, and was one of the firmest bases of scientific belief, that the world was symmetrical. That every action produces a particular reaction, that although mass can change into energy, and vice versa, the total amount of mass-energy in the universe will always be the same.

This law of, or belief in, symmetry, formed the basis of scientific prediction. If the total amount of energy was conserved in the world and each action produced a reaction then the future could be determined in principle and the world would thus be a determinate place. But if there existed some divergence from the norm then the possibility of freedom was introduced. It would no longer be possible to work out, even in theory, what reactions would result from a specific action or experiment. It had been discovered already by Louis Pasteur that organic life was not physically symmetrical and that this was the basic difference between living and dead matter.

Now two Chinese-born physicists, Chen Ning Yang and Tsung Dao Lee discovered that there was no evidence for the conservation of parity in weak interactions. On the basis of this hypothesis Madam Chien-Shiung Wu, professor of physics at Columbia University, agreed to put that hypothesis to the test of a practical experiment.

The experiment was performed on beta-decay of cobalt-60. In the weak interaction beta-particles were emitted from the north and south ends of the nuclei. The expectation was that there would be no difference in the average number of particles flung out from one end or the other. Wolfgang Pauli, eagerly awaiting the results, voiced the expectations of the scientific world: 'I do *not* believe that the Lord is a weak left-hander, and I am ready to bet a very high sum that the experiments will give symmetrical results.'[12] Professor Pauli lost his bet when it was seen that most of the particles were flung out from the south end.

The importance of this discovery was both general and particular. The particular importance lay in the fact that for the first time it was possible to distinguish between the north and south poles. The general importance lay in the fundamental realization that the world is not a completely symmetrical place.

There has been a tendency to argue that this general importance is not of any great moment, and now that the initial excitement has died down, the shock with which the discovery was originally greeted has been moderated. Scientists quite rightly point out that the weak interaction is the one we know least about and it is probably the least important of the four forces now known. And it may well be that apart from telling the difference between the north and south poles, the discovery has had no other practical significance.

But that, surely, is to miss the point. So far as the general significance of the discovery is concerned, the point is that an exception has been found to the previously held view of the world as a totally symmetrical place. From the philosophical point of view it is clear that the world as it was seen before this discovery is no longer the same. That view no longer represents reality as we now know it. The importance is that an element of freedom has been introduced on the physical level and it is this fact which is of the most vital importance in understanding the nature of matter and the world in which we live.

4 THE MAGICAL UNIVERSE – THE VOID

Having looked briefly at the discoveries that scientists have made, we can now turn to their conclusions. Of what is the physical world composed, the Moon that we see in the sky, our own human bodies, and the Earth on which we live? And what has happened to the assumptions upon which the scientists' search has been made?

The assumption that there is some kind of fundamental building block from which the universe is created remains. In view of the work of quantum physicists, it might be thought that the belief in a tangible basis for this building block could no longer be maintained, but here scientists are divided. And to a great extent the continuing argument about whether the atom, and thus matter as a whole, is made up of particles or waves, demonstrates this schism.

The temptation simply to push down the level of the building block one step further once it was discovered that the atom was not itself the ultimate constituent matter, has proved strong with certain scientists. It was perhaps not unreasonable to regard the protons and electrons as minute pieces of matter because at times electrons do act like particles rather than waves. Now that the atom has been broken down into the so-called fundamental particles, the very name of these entities illustrates the assumption of materiality.

In a recent report in *Nature* it was stated:

> One of the most exhaustive experiments by particle physicists has ended with the discovery of one of the tiniest building blocks of matter. It is called the sixth quark.... The everyday world can now be explained in terms of the family of quarks in one group of basic building blocks and a family of leptons in another.[13]

Other scientists prefer to see the atom as an electronic pattern composed of positive and negative charges, and thus to say that the universe is made up of electricity or electromagnetic waves. This was the view of Sir James Jeans who stated: 'We live in a universe of waves and nothing but waves.'

Whether one sees the basis of matter as particles or waves, the idea of a basic building block is retained. In the latter case the basic building block is one electromagnetic wave which travels at a constant speed. Quantum theory is incorporated into this view with the quantum energy made up of whole numbers times the wave period. Thus the speed of the waves is the same, but the frequency varies depending on the value of whole numbers. According to this view, matter is made up of the pattern of the waves which forms the atoms. The electromagnetic spectrum represents the basic pattern in the universe and exists independently of us. Physical phenomena as we see them exist in the way we interact with this pattern. We see a part of it as physical manifestation because we are tuned into a certain frequency, we hear part of it because we are tuned into another part.

In this division of opinion, or viewpoint, we have seen that one of the assumptions made by scientists has been abandoned. The tangible basis of matter is no longer accepted by all scientists, and indeed we have seen that Einstein cast aside this idea in his field theory when he stated that there was no longer any room for both the field and matter.

The assumption of a fundamental building block has been precariously maintained although it has been on shaky ground ever since the atom was broken down. The assumption that the universe obeys definite laws disappears completely at the sub-atomic level for it is clear that the fundamental particles, if indeed they exist, do not conform to definite rules. As Norbert Wiener put it: 'Thus chance has been admitted, not merely as a mathematical tool for physics, but as part of its warp and weft.'[14]

But a compromise can be reached here. Although certainty breaks down at the sub-atomic level, at the everyday level a pattern can be seen. The structure remains intact, although the individual goes its own way. This has led scientists like Willard Gibbs to put forward the idea of a contingent universe, one that is neither determinate nor indeterminate, but that is predictable only within statistical limits.

Not all scientists, however, have been prepared to relinquish their preconceived ideas so readily. In particular the idea of uncertainty at the quantum level led Einstein to assert that quantum theory must be untrue because it contravened the assumption of determinism.

The assumption that a thing can only be one thing at a time is so firmly rooted in the scientific mind, that it has become a mental block. The final assumption, that the world of matter is objective, has proved more insidious. The separation between the world 'out there' and those who observe it has been one of the basic tenets of scientific research.

With the advent of quantum physics that view is no longer

tenable. The observer is now an integral part of the world he views and becomes a participator. But in spite of the apparent acceptance of this principle, it is clear that the underlying assumption of separation remains, and it is this which has proved to be one of the most difficult barriers to surmount.

This was another assumption that Einstein was not prepared to abandon, and it was brought to light in an experiment which he devised to prove that quantum theory was incorrect. This experiment also goes to the root of the dilemma between causation and synchronicity. For if one thing is caused by another, then separateness is assumed. The driver of a car can only cause an accident and collide with a pedestrian if he and the pedestrian are two separate entities.

In 1935 Einstein collaborated with Nathan Rosen and Boris Podolsky in what came to be known as the Einstein–Rosen–Podolsky paradox or simply the E–R–P paradox. The basis of the experiment was that an atom, on its decay, would send two photons simultaneously towards two parallel polarizers.

As soon as an observation was made on one photon, the second photon immediately assumed a similar value. It appears, therefore, that there is an instantaneous signal from one photon to the other. Now the polarizers can be placed at any distance from each other, even light years away. Still, one polarizer immediately assumes the value of the other. This appears to mean that a communication is being made from one photon to the other faster than the speed of light, which is impossible because it infringes the relativity laws that Einstein laid down. Not only is there no causal connection between the two photons but the whole principle of causation is threatened. For the observation of one photon could be made after the other photon had reached its destination, and so the arrow of time would be reversed. On the accepted principles of causation, the observation of one photon would cause something which had already happened. Einstein's purpose was to show that quantum theory was nonsense, but if one looks at the situation with an open mind, it could equally be held that quantum theory was correct and that Einstein's assumptions were wrong.

It is indeed difficult to see how an observation of one object can affect another object after that object has already acted in a certain way. But that is just because of the underlying assumption that the connection between the two objects is one of causation which in turn assumes separation.

Many scientists have shifted their view of reality to an underlying pattern which is made up by the individual particles. Paul Davies has put forward the theory that as each musical instrument produces a characteristic sound, so does each atom produce a characteristic spectrum of light. 'We can,' he says, 'therefore regard the spectrum of light from an atom as similar to the pattern of sound from a musical instrument.' He goes on: 'In both cases there is a deep association between the internal vibrations (oscillating membranes, undulating electron waves) and the external waves (sound, light).'[15]

The same idea has recently been put forward in the field of biology by Dr Rupert Sheldrake. According to his view there is a physical field pattern which links or connects the whole world. So when a new development or line of evolution occurs in a species a pattern is created in the world as a whole. The more this physical pattern of behaviour is repeated the stronger the resonance becomes. As he says: 'The persistence of material forms depends on a continuously repeated actualisation of the system under the influence of its morphogenetic field; at the same time the morphogenetic field is continuously re-created by morphic resonance from similar past forms.'[16] Of course this places the emphasis more on a strictly physical structure than on an underlying wave pattern, but the basic principle is the same.

Similarly, David Bohm has advocated the idea of structure:

> One is led to a new notion of unbroken wholeness which denies the classical idea of analysability of the world into separately and independently existing parts... We have reversed the usual classical notion that the independent 'elementary' parts of the world are the fundamental reality, and that the various systems are merely particular contingent forms and arrangements of those parts. Rather, we say that inseparable quantum interconnectedness of the whole universe is the fundamental reality, and that relatively independently behaving parts are merely particular and contingent forms within this whole.[17]

Werner Heisenberg made the attempt to dispense with both

the models of physical particles and wave patterns in his description of the atom. He depicted the energy level or orbits of the electrons simply in terms of number. But although he was awarded the Nobel Prize for physics in 1932 for his work, his theory of matrix mechanics did not succeed in taking over from the more graphic descriptions.

At the beginning of this chapter I alluded to the primal symbol of Astrology, the circle with the dot in the centre. The tendency has been for scientists to view the world from the outside, from the circle. And this is natural enough for science is concerned with the material world.

Because they have found no tangible basis for the world, these scientists have concluded that the world is an illusion; it is something which we have dreamed. And thus they have sought to equate physics with mysticism. But there is a vital difference between the view of the mystic and that of the physicist.

The physicist believes only in tangible reality and when he finds that the basis of matter is insubstantial he believes that the world does not exist. But the mystic believes that the intangible is everything. Although they have both reached the Void, for the scientist it is the end, while for the mystic it is the beginning.

Yet others accept that there are different laws in the subatomic world from those that appear to govern the everyday realm. But they make no attempt to equate or integrate the two. Thus they live in a divided world where the centre is separated from the circumference. They fail to appreciate the basic truth that the world consists of both levels.

The danger of the astrologer basing his views on those of the scientist should now be apparent. If astrologers make the same assumptions as scientists then they will inevitably end up in the same blind alleys. This is not to impugn science in itself. The work that scientists have done and the discoveries that they have made are as fascinating as they are necessary. And it is only with the help of science that the basis of the physical world will be discovered.

Science was originally called in because its methods were needed. They are still needed. But they are needed not in isolation but in conjunction with a wider understanding and it is a mistake to think that science is based on objective fact. As

Karl Popper has written in *The Logic of Scientific Discovery*: 'Scientific discovery is impossible without faith in ideas which are of a purely speculative kind, and sometimes even quite hazy; a faith which is completely unwarranted from the point of view of science, and which, to that extent, is "metaphysical" '.

CHAPTER 3
Heaven and Earth – the world of the magician

> Heaven and earth shall pass away: but my words shall not pass away.
>
> Mark 13.31

In the last chapter we looked at the world through the eyes of the scientist. In this chapter we shall look at the world through the eyes of the magician or occultist. From the surface we now move closer to the centre and from the centre we can see what appeared to be the surface in a new way.

Niels Bohr defined reality as whatever can be weighed or measured. And in doing so he cut himself off from the centre and from half of reality. As we have seen, this view has not been shared by many of his fellow scientists who appreciated that they had to include themselves in any total view of reality. The scientist as observer of an objective world was dead. Instead he had become a participator in an integral part of the universe.

Scientists have come to realize that matter is affected by the mind. Magicians have realized all along that matter is mind. Heaven and Earth are but two aspects of the same world. It is only because of the way our minds are formed that we see the two separately.

That is why the astrologer is in a unique position. For he, and he almost alone, can see both worlds – separate yet one. But in order to see the two, the astrologer must himself learn to see like both the scientist and the magician. He needs to incorporate the models of both as the foundation of his art.

1 THE SPIRITUAL WORLD

> Real are the dreams of Gods, and smoothly pass
> Their pleasures in a long immortal dream.
>
> John Keats

Let us first clarify just what we mean by the spiritual world. As a matter of convenience, I have so far talked of two worlds – the material and the spiritual. But this division is incomplete, for the spiritual level should really be confined to only a part of what lies beyond the material.

The worlds of the magician are four – the material, the astral, the higher mental and the spiritual, ascending in that order from earth up to heaven. These four worlds are separate just as the sub-atomic world is separate from the material world, and in the same way, different laws apply to the different realms.

But, also like the sub-atomic and the material, they are the same world. It is not easy to look at the different levels simultaneously because we have been taught to see only in three dimensions. Nevertheless the four levels co-exist just as a table exists as a material object and also as an innumerable number of interacting particles reaching out to each other on another level.

The level we are most readily in touch with is the physical world. As well as the world of matter as we know it, this level also includes the etheric world. The etheric constitutes a mirror-image of the physical on a subtler level. All living organisms possess an etheric body which pulsates like a radiating luminous covering at a certain rate which is the energy field of the organism.

Occultists also call the etheric body the aura and, because it reflects the physical body, it can be used by spiritual healers to diagnose illness. Dr Harold Saxton Burr of Yale University school of medicine has called these electrodynamic fields, which appear to organize the structure of living entities, 'L-fields'. These 'L-fields' form the blueprint of the organism which keeps the basic pattern intact while the actual materials change. So any portion of the L-field contains the entire design of the organism and, therefore, if the cells in the embryo are divided into half, each half will develop into a completely formed organism.

Because the etheric world is so much more subtle than the physical, one popular misconception is to associate it with the astral level. Often the terms 'astral travel' and the 'astral body' refer to what is in reality etheric travel and the etheric body.

In etheric travel the mirror-image is separated from the physical body and the consciousness transferred to the etheric body, and it is this form which we enter involuntarily in dreams. This entity is also the 'ghost' which is sometimes left behind when the physical body dies.

The etheric body can be sensed with our normal five senses as well as with a 'sixth sense' in the form of atmosphere, but usually it takes someone with finely tuned senses to see it. The etheric plane as a whole may be thought of as a grid of force whose basic structure holds together the physical world as we know it, or like a vast spider's web which pervades the universe but which is invisible to those whose sight is not acute.

The next level is the astral world. This is the level of the imagination where most magical work is done, and it is part of the world of the Mind, which is quite separate from the physical world. If we look at Figure 3.1 we can see the mental plane, consisting of the astral and the higher mental, mediating between the spiritual and the physical.

The dividing line between the physical and the astral is the one that materialists conceive of as separating reality from the imagination. This, of course, depends on one's definition of reality. If the definition of Niels Bohr is taken as consisting of what can only be weighed or measured, then the world of the astral must be excluded.

The astral plane is that which is built up by people's thoughts, whether they be deliberate or unconscious. For every thought that emanates from the human mind is imprinted on the astral and can be read in the Akashic records. Most of these thoughts are so weak that their impression is negligible. Others are so potent that they create great forces. In this way the god forms have been built up and nurtured by group minds, and so the power of the planetary energies has been created. Anyone can produce a personal astral form by using his creative imagination.

This form becomes the astral body which is the reflection of the individual's desires and so it has also been called the Desire Body. The difference between the etheric and the astral body can now readily be seen, for the astral body can take any shape

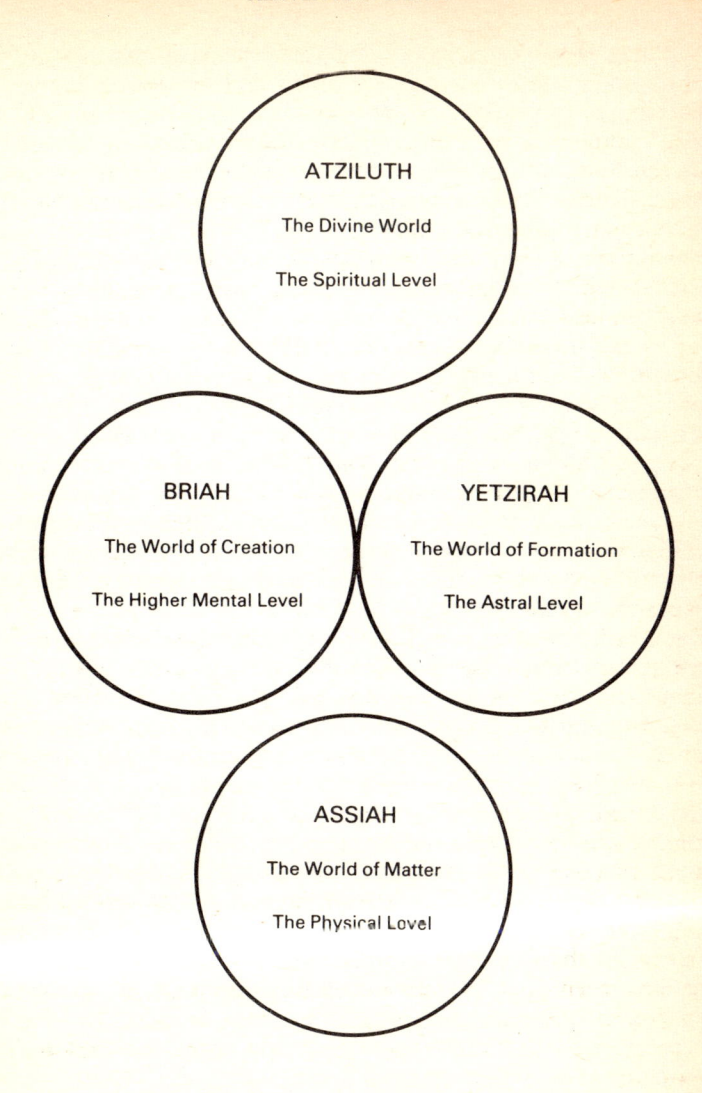

Figure 3.1 *The four levels of existence*

that a person wishes, consciously or unconsciously, while the etheric body will always resemble his physical shape.

Because thoughts are projected onto the astral plane, atmospheres pervade certain places, depending on the force of the imagination at work. Where men and women have worshipped over long periods, the atmosphere is particularly strong. And the aura of the place is continued by people worshipping the particular God that is the creation of their minds. 'Where there are two or three gathered together in my name, there am I in the midst of them.'[1]

Normally the astral body moves only on the astral plane, but the trained occultist can make it manifest on the material plane, just as the Gods can be made visible on the physical plane. In this case there must be a physical vehicle for the astral or god body. Thoughts then are real even though they are not material. Thought is energy and as has been increasingly demonstrated in the investigation of psychokinesis and spiritual healing, the link between mind and matter can no longer be ignored.

The higher mental world is part of the realm of the mind along with the astral plane. The role of the mind is different on this level from that of the astral, however, for the Higher Mind is more akin to eastern thought and seeks a more direct link with the spiritual in the form of mysticism and meditation, while the astral concentrates on imagination and creative thought, and is therefore more appropriate for the western mentality.

Finally, we come to the spiritual world. This is the level of archetypes, of basic principles. The world of the absolute, of God Himself. It is not possible to contact this level directly in this incarnation. The highest we can reach is the astral or the higher mental. The two mental levels then are the realm of the soul governed by the Moon and they are a half-way house between Heaven and Earth.

We have to proceed through the realm of the soul in order to reach higher. While on Earth we can only approach the spiritual through a mediator for no one can see the face of God and live. 'I am the way, the truth, and the life: no man cometh unto the Father, but by me.'[2] It is therefore important not to confuse the soul with the spirit. The astral should reflect the spiritual, just as the Moon reflects the Sun.

As Meister Eckhart put it:

> The masters say that for me to know anything, it must be fully present to me and like my understanding. The saints say potentiality is in the Father, likeness in the Son, and unity in the Holy Ghost. Therefore since the Father is wholly present in the Son and the Son is wholly like him, none knows the Father save the Son.[3]

The principle works both ways. Instead of reflecting God or our spiritual nature, we can simply see the reflection of our own minds and mistake that for God. That is what happens with so many fanatics and fundamentalists who believe they are seeing God, while in reality they see only the inflation of their own egos.

When the diviner, be he astrologer, tarot reader or ritual magician, attempts to see into the future, what he contacts is the astral or higher mental plane, and not the spiritual. The failure to appreciate this fundamental point lies at the root of the widespread failure to understand the question of prediction, and we shall examine this problem in greater detail in chapter 5.

2 THE MODEL OF THE MAGICIAN – THE KABBALAH

> To him that overcometh will I give to eat of the tree of life, which is in the midst of the paradise of God.
>
> Revelations 2.7[4]

Just as science uses models, so does magic. Although their models are used in different ways, their purpose is the same. It is to see the reality behind the outer form. The way science uses its models is through the conscious mind. Its models are signs; they are used to communicate to the intellect more directly than written explanation.

Magic uses its models to get through to the unconscious. It uses symbols which have a deeper meaning than signs and which cannot be understood by rational analysis alone. They are also more comprehensive than scientific models. The prime model of western magic, the Kabbalah, is a model of the whole of reality, of the complete universe on every level.

Because the Kabbalah is a visual, symbolic system it is ideal for the western mind. In recent years eastern ideas have been increasingly appropriated by westerners and much insight has been gained in this way. But there is a basic difference in the way the western and the eastern mind functions.

The reality behind both is the same. The gods in western pantheons are represented by similar ones in the east. The great universal truths contained in mythology the world over are the same. But the approach is different. The eastern mind prefers the route of direct union and tends to be more abstract, while that of the west is more attuned to material forms and works better with visual symbolism and ritual. Therefore for westerners, the astral plane is the more appropriate level for the magician, while the easterner finds the higher mental the more natural path. Of course, neither the astral nor the higher mental is any better or 'higher' than the other. Inevitably, where a horizontal model is used, one must be placed higher than the other and, to redress that tendency, I have placed the two side by side in Figure 3.1.

The basic model in the system of the Kabbalah is the Tree of Life. In the story of Adam and Eve in Genesis, the first human couple ate of the Tree of Knowledge of Good and Evil. With the emphasis so much on that tree it is sometimes overlooked that there was another tree in the garden. 'And out of the ground made the Lord God to grow every tree that is pleasant to the sight, and good for food, the tree of life also in the midst of the garden, and the tree of knowledge of good and evil.'[5]

Having eaten the fruit of one tree, God made sure that the pair would not be able to taste of the other.

> And the Lord God said, Behold the man is become as one of us, to know good and evil, and now, lest he put forth his hand, and take also of the tree of life, and eat, and live for ever: Therefore the Lord God sent him forth from the garden of Eden.[6]

David Conway has called the Tree of Life: 'A mystical vision of the ultimate reality behind the world of form.'[7] It consists of a series of emanations, of ten principles which together represent the four worlds of the occultist I described in the last section. These ten principles are named Sephiroth and are represented by numbers which correspond to the Hebrew letters.

There are two principles operating here. First there are the sephiroth themselves which symbolize specific types of energy, much like the planets in Astrology. Second, there are the four levels which are operative in each of the sephiroth. So each sephira functions on the four planes we described in the last section.

Thus each sephira contains in its highest level the world of Atziluth, the spiritual plane, the Divine or archetypal world of emanations. Then Briah, the higher mental or creative world. Then Yetzirah, corresponding to the astral plane, or the world of formation. Finally, Assiah is reached, the physical level or the world of action.

The four worlds are effective in each principle. To take an example, in writing this book, there was first the original seed, the idea on the Atziluth level. Then came the working out of the creative idea in the imagination, then the modelling into structure and form, and finally the completed, published work.

The sephiroth themselves should be seen both as separate principles and also in relation to each other. The Tree of Life is ideal Man, Adam Kadmon, or anything else in its ideal aspect – the universe or God. It is the basic structure or pattern of life, and all existence is built upon its form.

One can work with the Tree by starting at the top or at the bottom, just as one can look at the human body by examining first the head or the feet. Eventually we learn to see the body as a whole and the tree as a whole, the former connected by the bones, muscles and tissues and the latter by the related paths.

The combination of separateness and relatedness can be seen most readily when we look at the principles at their most fundamental level, as numbers. Each number contains its own meaning, but the lower numbers are also contained in the higher. Thus the 2 has meaning as 2, but it also contains the meaning of the 1. In this way life becomes more complex as one works down the Tree. When we arrive at the 10 we reach the ultimate complexity encompassing all the previous numbers.

The relationship between the principles can be visualized more readily because each is placed on one of three pillars, and each is connected by one of the twenty-two paths, corresponding to the major arcana of the tarot, as illustrated in Figure 3.2. Strictly speaking, there are only two pillars, the Left and the Right, which form the world of duality as we know it. These represent the opposing forces of positive and negative, male and female, yang and yin, catabolic and anabolic. The so-called middle pillar represents equilibrium or the principle of balance between the two.

It would take a book in itself to describe the principles of the Kabbalah in detail and many excellent books have been written on the subject. Here I shall briefly outline the basic meanings of the sephiroth together with their astrological correspondences.

The first sephira is Kether, the Crown, whose number is 1. This is the absolute, Godhead, and it bears no astrological correspondence. But behind this sephira there is another principle. Before there can be anything, there must be nothing. Here is encapsulated the whole problem of material creation and physical reality. What is the nature of this no thing that we call nothing? Is it in fact nothing or is it something?

Science has no answer to this vital question. Because science has made the assumption that there is a tangible basis to the world, it can get no farther back than the number 1. Behind this number, material existence as we know it ceases to exist. The scientist is then faced with the choice of either rejecting the material world as illusion or of clinging to tangible manifestation.

But the occultist, and the mystic, knows that behind the Manifest there is the Unmanifest. Behind the veil of existence which is represented by the number 1, is the void, represented by 0. And, far from being nothing, the kabbalist divides this realm into three phases: Ain, darkness; Ain Soph, limitless light, and finally, Ain Soph Aur, limited light. 'All things are created out of nothing,' said Meister Eckhart. 'Therefore their true source is nothing.'[8]

Figure 3.2 *The Tree of Life with the sephiroth and the major arcana of the Tarot on the paths*

HEAVEN AND EARTH

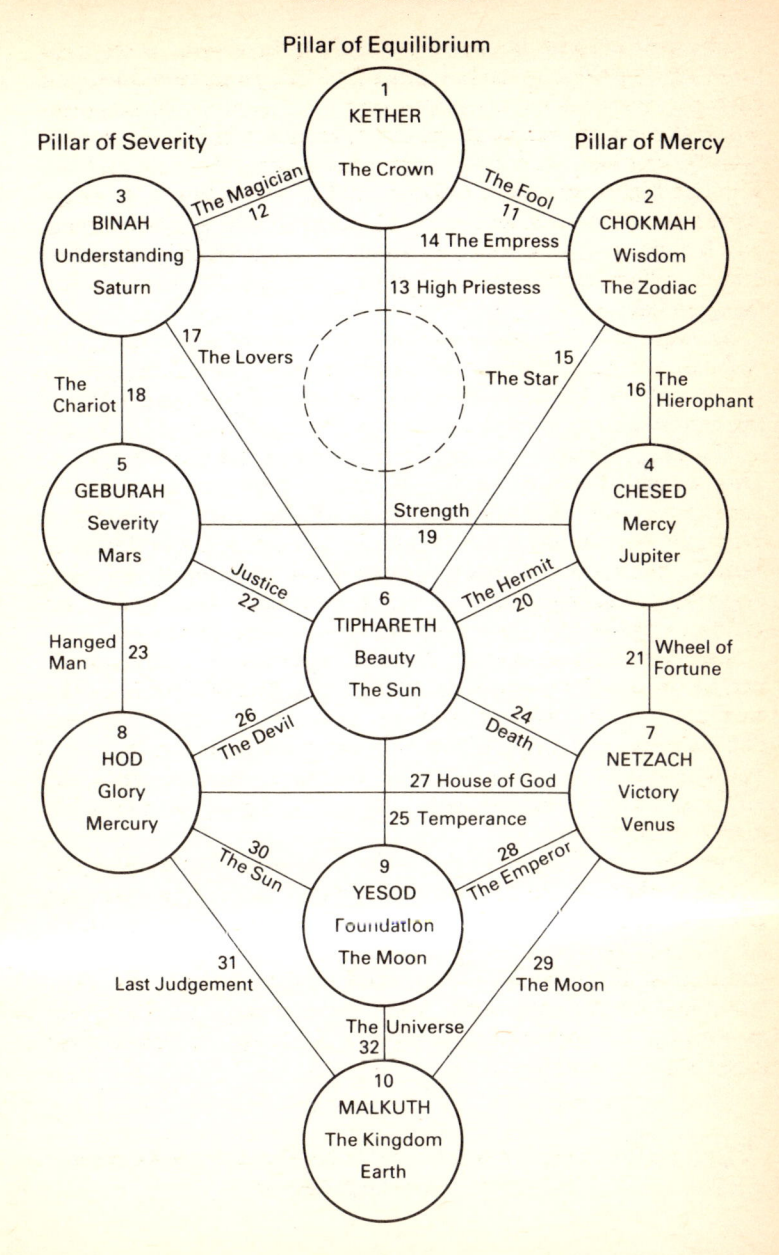

Pillar of Equilibrium

Pillar of Severity   **Pillar of Mercy**

1 KETHER — The Crown

3 BINAH — Understanding — Saturn

2 CHOKMAH — Wisdom — The Zodiac

12 The Magician
11 The Fool
14 The Empress
13 High Priestess

17 The Lovers
15 The Star
18 The Chariot
16 The Hierophant

5 GEBURAH — Severity — Mars

4 CHESED — Mercy — Jupiter

19 Strength
22 Justice
20 The Hermit
21 Wheel of Fortune

6 TIPHARETH — Beauty — The Sun

23 Hanged Man
26 The Devil
24 Death

8 HOD — Glory — Mercury

7 NETZACH — Victory — Venus

27 House of God
25 Temperance
30 The Sun
28 The Emperor

9 YESOD — Foundation — The Moon

31 Last Judgement
29 The Moon

32 The Universe

10 MALKUTH — The Kingdom — Earth

Kether heads the top of the central pillar and is at the apex of the whole Tree. Here is unity, eternity, perfection. The still point at the centre of the whirling world. When God the Absolute looks at Himself, when He reflects upon His perfection, the principle of duality is born and perfection itself is ended. The universe as we know it, has come into being, opposition and paradox are created. The second sephira, Chokmah, is associated with the wheel of the Zodiac or the sphere of the Fixed Stars. To quote David Conway again: 'The Universe is God's awareness of himself.' Enlil has cut the mountain into two.

Binah, the third sephira, corresponding to Saturn, the Great Mother of the Universe, Ama, mother of sorrows, heads the left-hand pillar, just as Chokmah heads the right. These first three sephiroth form the Supernal Triangle, the abode of the spirit. God ruling the world with Christ at His right hand and Satan at His left. This sphere can only be reached by crossing the chasm of the invisible sephira named Daath.

Chesed, corresponding to Jupiter, is the next sephira and is below Chokmah on the pillar of Mercy. Opposing, and balancing it, is Geburah, the outgoing force of Mars. The sixth sephira, Tiphareth, the Sun, is the centre of the whole Tree, and lies in the middle of the central pillar. Between Kether and Yesod it forms the link between spirit and soul.

The Sun is also the Son, the mediator between God and Man. 'No man hath ascended up to heaven, but he that came down from heaven, even the Son of man which is in heaven.'[9] And because we cannot reach the spiritual world direct, we need the Son to see the Father. 'Ye shall seek me, and shall not find me: and where I am, thither ye cannot come.'[10]

The seventh sephira is Netzach corresponding to Venus, and it opposes Hod, Mercury, the concrete or lower mind. With the ninth sephira, Yesod, the Moon, on the middle pillar, there is formed the triangle which is equivalent to the astral plane and it is these three principles which are of particular importance when dealing with magical techniques.

The final sephira, Malkuth, represents the Earth and the physical world and naturally forms the basis of the Tree. While it does not correspond to any astrological factor directly unless one takes into account the diurnal circle of the Horoscope, it does serve to remind us that the physical level is very much a part of reality as a whole. We always need to look at the spiritual and the other intermediate levels with our feet firmly on the ground.

It should be apparent from this brief survey that Astrology and the Kabbalah are inextricably linked. Indeed they are really two aspects of one system and should be used to complement each other. We can see universal man on the Tree and the individual in the Horoscope. If we want to understand the principle of Mars, for instance, we need to look at Geburah on the Tree as a principle both in itself and also in relation to the other sephiroth which correspond to the remaining astrological factors.

Having understood the nature of Mars as a general attribute in the context of the psyche as a whole, we can then go on to look at the Horoscope to see how it will operate on the individual level, much as the doctor needs to understand the human body through the study of anatomy before he examines the individual patient.

3 MIND – THE MISSING LINK

We have looked at Earth and we have looked at Heaven. The scientist says that reality exists only in the material realm. The spiritual world is not real. Either it does not exist at all, or it exists only in the imagination, which amounts to the same thing.

The mystic takes the opposite view, it is the physical world which is unreal. It is maya, illusion. The real world is that of the spirit. We are not of our bodies, not even of our minds. We can get away from our bodies and away from our concrete, conscious minds by practising meditation. Then we experience true reality by reaching our spiritual level.

The magician encompasses both levels. His model contains both body and spirit as integral parts of one reality. If we look at the first card in the major arcana of the tarot, the number 1, we see the Magician with one hand pointing up to heaven, and the other directed down towards the earth. The Magician is Mercury and symbolizes the mind and from his mind he creates the world. He stands in the middle of the magic circle, the dot in the centre of the Horoscope, and weaves the circumference of material existence. In one sense this world of ours is an illusion, it is maya. It depends upon us for its existence and it changes with each successive moment of time. It is the projection of our minds.

In another sense the world we live in is real. However much it changes, it always remains our world. The magician is also the magus, the wise man who came to worship the infant Jesus. And as the number 1, he is God the Absolute. As Dion Fortune has written: 'The Universe is really a thought form projected from the mind of God.'[11]

The idea of the world as a manifestation of the mind of God through the spoken word is current in the majority of the ancient mythologies. For the power of the magician is the word. 'In the beginning was the Word, and the Word was with God, and the Word was God.'[12]

According to the Egyptians the world was created by the dynamic power called Hike, or magic, which they also named Thota, as the expression of their chief god, Thoth, who corresponded to Mercury. According to Anglo-Saxon belief, the Gods themselves were bound by the power of the Wyrd, containing the essence both of the word and of magic. This principle, being equivalent to Fate or Necessity, was decided by the Norns.

For the magician both Heaven and Earth are real. They are but two aspects of the same essence. The problem that the scientist faces is that in accepting the physical level alone as real he cannot understand the implications of the lower level he has himself reached through quantum mechanics.

In quantum physics the effects of virtual particle production can be seen. Massive particles emerge from the empty void between particles and then disappear again into the void. Things, material things, are thus apparently created out of nothing. It should be clear to scientists now, as it has always been to occultists, that there is no such thing as nothing.

There is only the manifest and the unmanifest – the Ain Soph and Kether. Physical reality is not created out of nothing. It is contained in what we call nothing. But this 'nothing' is as real as the material which emerges from it. In the east it is called 'ch'i' – the potential energy from which everything is formed.

Thus creation on the material level is the actualization of the potential contained in this 'ch'i' or Ain Soph. The archetypal level, the essence, spirit or seed at the Atziluth level, materializes through the stages of manifestation into the Assiah or material level.

To devalue the power of the mind is to refuse to face reality. Anything that exists on the material level began its life on the mental plane. Action begins in ideas. The visions of Napoleon, Hitler, Lawrence of Arabia were contained initially in their minds. The thoughts of the son of a village carpenter in an obscure middle eastern land changed the face of the world.

In India fakirs walk on red-hot coals whose surface temperature exceeds 900 degrees fahrenheit and whose interior temperature exceeds 2,500 degrees fahrenheit. Yogis sit naked on the mountainside on winter nights drying sheets dipped in icy water from the heat generated by their mental processes.

The occultist and the scientist both use the mind in different ways. The scientist through the conscious faculties and the occultist through the unconscious. But scientists are gradually becoming more aware of the deeper levels of reality. As Max Planck has said: 'Science... means unresting endeavour and continually progressing development towards an aim which the poetic intuition may apprehend, but which the intellect can never fully grasp.'[13]

The magician sees the universe as a multitude of lines, criss-crossing each other, forming a vast pattern, like a gigantic spider's web. The four levels, the spiritual, creative, formative and material, co-exist on these lines and the magician transposes one to the other.

When he travels in his etheric body he uses the etheric stresses that exist. When he travels in the astral body, he uses his creative imagination, the power of his mind. But he does not create something out of nothing. To create something, an idea or a character, he contacts the highest plane – the level of Atziluth, the archetypal essence.

In terms of the human psyche the astral plane is equivalent to the collective unconscious, using Jung's terminology, and the spiritual level to the archetypes. To a great extent the psychologist has now taken over the magician's work. The difference is that the magician has personalized the various factors in the form of the gods, calling the principle of assertiveness and anger, Mars; and that of structure and isolation, Saturn.

As Israel Regardie has written:

> Magic concerns itself in the main with the world of modern psychology, that is to say, it deals on that sphere of the psyche of which normally we are not conscious but which exerts an enormous influence upon our lives. Magic is a series of psychological techniques so devised as to enable us to probe more deeply into ourselves.[14]

The magician creates a form by contacting the Atziluth level and working on the astral level. He then either brings the form down to the material level or leaves it to be contacted by later minds using the same process. Thus from the collective unconscious have been projected unto the constellations the forms of the Signs of the Zodiac and the planets through telesmatic images, and these are filled with a group power that enables others to get in touch with their essence.

4 THE SYMBOLIC UNION – THE ASTROLOGER AS MAGICIAN

> A knowledge of the gods is accompanied with . . . the knowledge of ourselves.
>
> IAMBLICHUS

Just as the material and the spiritual levels are united by the mind, so science and magic are united by Astrology. The dilemma that faces Astrology today, the choice between science and the occult as its basis, is resolved once it is appreciated that both scientists and occultists are looking at precisely the same world, and it is only their terminology which differs.

This world of ours is quite literally a magical world. The old science looked only at the circumference, the world of classic physics, the material realm. Now with the advent of quantum physics, science has also arrived at the centre, the still point where existence is a dance of energy.

That some of the more progressive scientists are now

beginning to appreciate that the world they see is the same as the world that is viewed by those in other disciplines is apparent from remarks such as these: 'There is a deep underlying connection between the fields of physics, mathematics, philosophy (including metaphysics, epistemology, and ethics) astrology, art, music, religion, psychology, mythology and language.'[15]

The models of science and magic are different. The world these models describe are the same. The approach to this reality is equally different for science and magic use the mind in different ways, science relying mainly on the rational faculty to explain, and magic relying more on the intuition to understand.

Here too the astrologer seeks to see reality as a whole by using his rational and intuitive faculties together. This is far from being an easy task but it is a necessary one if we are to explain and experience both the spiritual and material levels.

For both levels are contained in us. We are formed of the spirit, and in the world. To be whole people we need to live on both levels at once. If we are centred, we are in touch with our spiritual nature. Then we are in Tao, in a state of grace, and we need only listen to the still voice that dwells in the centre to know all things. Then science, magic and Astrology blend into the one they are, and explanation can be understood. Then, too, we can experience both inner and outer. 'Magic', in the words of Gareth Knight, 'is practical scientific experience of an inner nature.'[16] The four levels that we have described need to be experienced otherwise they appear to be separate physical places rather than states that co-exist.

This is why symbols are used. For symbols incorporate a graphic description, and at the same time lead us to experience the inner meaning behind the outer form with our intuitive faculties.

Let us begin with explanation. We have seen that, according to the scientist's view of the universe, reality at the sub-atomic level is made up of electrical waves which are part of the electromagnetic spectrum. These waves are governed by specific quantum numbers. Here we see a vast pattern of waves radiating and interpenetrating throughout the universe, all reaching out to each other. These waves all travel at the same speed, 186,000 miles a second, and their frequency changes depending on the amount of energy contained in them.

The occultist's world, too, is made up of a pattern of stresses like tramlines which form both the etheric and the astral planes. For manifestation to occur, the condensation of the unmanifest has to enter one of the channels according to a specific number. This is what happens when the sub-atomic particles appear to the scientist, and when the magician brings a force into manifestation.

Each object and element in nature has a particular rate of vibration and the art of the magician is to tune himself in with the particular vibration through the correct sound or mantra. It is this use of vibration in sound that formed the word which originally created the world. Just as sound shatters glass and patterns are formed in the sand with a violin, so the magician uses his power to mould the plastic substance of the astral light or akaysha into various shapes and forms. As Dion Fortune has written: 'The art of the magician ... lies in aligning himself with cosmic force in order that the operation he desires to perform may come about as a part of the working of cosmic activities.'[17]

At the sub-atomic level matter as we know it ceases to exist. And because it cannot be seen or touched many scientists deny its existence. Whether it is regarded as 'real' or not, nature at the quantum level is equivalent to the astral level and to the unconscious. It, too, is a state of being rather than a physical place.

We cannot see the inner world directly. Sometimes we get glimpses of it, but the simplicity of view is lost to most of us as we grow older and lose our innocence, although it is retained by some mystics and poets. As St Paul said: 'When I was a child, I understood as a child: but when I became a man, I put away childish things. For now we see through a glass, darkly; but then, face to face: now I know in part; but then shall I know even as I am known.'[18]

Because we cannot see directly into the inner worlds, we need some formal representation. The pure spirit, the archetype, is inaccessible to our minds and therefore we create an emotionally charged illustration in the form of a symbol, so that we are led back to the abstract source, and the finite mind is merged with the infinite. Thus the symbol reveals the inner meaning by bringing the abstract into concrete form as an image.

It does not matter what symbol we use provided it is meaningful to us. Naturally different symbols will appeal to different temperaments. The symbol points inward like language and, like language, it is the meaning that matters – not whether French, German, Russian or Hungarian is used. As Jung has said: 'Whether you call the principle of existence "God", "matter", "energy", or anything else you like, you have created nothing; you have simply changed a symbol.'

That is why the ancients believed that the gods were the constellations. The planets were our guides and the interpreters of these gods. So symbols are the language of mythology, magic and astrology, as well as psychology and science. For the material world is just as much a symbol as the more obvious forms of the Cross and the Horoscope. 'We might say that the archetype as such is concentrated psychic energy,' writes Whitmont, 'but that the symbol provides the mode of manifestation by which the archetype becomes discernible.'[19]

One main reason for reality not being understood is because people use their rational minds. This is why scientists fail to understand the meaning of the universe. In failing to appreciate that matter is symbolic, they ask the wrong questions and cannot find the answers.

This is also why many astrologers fail to understand the meaning behind a Horoscope. They, too, use their rational minds and in doing so their conscious theoretical knowledge uses the image as a substitute for the real experience. The images should emerge spontaneously from the unconscious, for that is where meaning resides.

This is a very real trap for astrologers. The symbols used in Astrology are a door to get through to the unconscious, inner world. They are taken from mythology and have tremendous power because their images have been built up telesmatically by generations of minds over thousands of years. In themselves the symbols are nothing. It is the force that lies behind them that counts. Nor are they necessary. The mystic achieves union with God more directly through the higher mental level. He takes the middle path instead of the serpent's way. The eastern mind, too, prefers the more direct route of meditation. If one is going to use symbols, and they are more natural for the western mind, they must be used properly.

As Oswald Wirth has written: 'By their very nature the symbols must remain elastic, vague and ambiguous, like the saying of an oracle. Their role is to unveil mysteries, leaving the mind all its freedom.' The same symbols are used by the astrologer and the magician, and indeed the two form part of one system.

In the words of Dion Fortune:

> The Tree of Life, Astrology and the tarot are not three mystical systems, but three aspects of one and the same system, and each is unintelligible without the others. It is only when we study Astrology on the basis of the Tree that we have a philosophical system.[20]

In the Birth Chart we see the forces contained within an individual. We can see, for example, how an individual's Mars will function, we can see its relationship to the other energies contained in that individual. We can tell whether this force, in this individual, is potentially frustrated, and if so, why and how. We can see the most appropriate ways in which it can be used. This is the essential diagnosis of a person's nature and Astrology performs an invaluable function in helping a person to understand himself.

But there are two things which Astrology in itself does not do, and it is here that it is complemented by the Kabbalah and the Tarot. The Tree shows us how the principle of Mars operates as a force most naturally in relation to the other forces on the Tree. So it enables us to understand the energy symbolized by Mars as an integral part of the whole person. While in the Birth Chart the factors are necessarily separated because we are dealing with an individual.

A problem which the astrologer constantly faces is how he can tell on which level a planetary force will manifest. As we have seen, a transit of Uranus may manifest on the physical level as a motor accident, or on a mental level as an interest in alchemy.

The second thing that can be achieved by magic is how to deal with the specific problems that are thrown up in a person's Horoscope. The purpose of magic is to get through to the gods, to get in touch with the unconscious. And it is by evoking the gods through Magic that the unconscious is stimulated.

To quote Dion Fortune again: 'Ceremonial, and especially telesmanic, magic is the essential complement of Astrology; for Astrology is the diagnosis of the trouble, but magic is the treatment of it by means of which the warring forces in our natures are equilibrated.'[21] By getting in touch with the force that Mars or Geburah represents we can transform its anger into strength, its fear into power, if the trouble lies in that direction.

By looking at each principle or sephira in terms of the other sephiroth this process of healing can be achieved as part of a whole operation. Geburah or Mars is not looked at in isolation but in relation to its opposite balancing force, Chesed or Jupiter. While we can see how the planets are related to each other by aspect in the Birth Chart, we can see the natural aspects between these forces in the twenty-two paths of the tarot major arcana which connect the ten sephiroth. Thus the Kabbalah represents the inner self, while the Birth Chart represents the outer person and his environment.

CHAPTER 4
The mystery of time

> And the angel which I saw stand upon the sea and upon the earth lifted up his hand to heaven, and sware by him that liveth for ever and ever ... that there should be time no longer: But in the days of the voice of the seventh angel, when he shall begin to sound, the mystery of God should be finished.
>
> Revelations 10.5

Michael Shallis, an astrophysicist, concluded a recent book on time by saying: 'Physically time is still unexplained.'[1] Scientists can perhaps get away with failing to understand time. Astrologers cannot. Time is the very basis of Astrology. The fundamental premise of Astrology is that the position of the heavenly bodies correlates with events on earth *at a particular time*. It is the fact that the planets form their pattern at *that time* which is the foundation of astrological theory.

Let us then try to understand the mystery of time. Let us begin by seeing how much, or how little, is known about this phenomenon. One of the problems with time is that it seems so simple until we start to think about it. Then it appears so complicated that we give up. We are tempted to agree with Charles Lamb when he said: 'Nothing puzzles me more than time and space: and yet nothing troubles me less, as I never think about them.'

The other problem is that we seem to be dealing with two different kinds of time. Time as we instinctively think of it appears to be constant. We live our lives from day to day and from year to year and we can measure this time with great accuracy. This is the way scientists in the past have seen time. But there is also the time of the mystic, the artist and the poet. Time that is eternal, that is more like a state of being than a continuous motion.

Are there, then, two kinds of time? And if so, what is the

connection between them? As we have seen, the thesis of this book is that the physical and the spiritual realm are the same, and the intersection between the timeless and time is symbolized in the Horoscope. The Horoscope is literally a moment of time and that moment of time describes two things: the physical pattern of the universe at that time, and the life of a human being or other entity throughout the whole of its life.

Astrology is the means to reconcile physical and spiritual time. In the symbolism of the Horoscope we see the convergence of the two. We see time as a whole. And we see that although time appears to be of two kinds, it is contained in a unified whole. We shall now look first at time as seen by the scientist and then as viewed by the mystic in order to reconcile the two.

1 TIME IN THE PHYSICAL WORLD

Absolute, true and mathematical time, of itself and from its own nature, flows equally without relation to anything external.
ISAAC NEWTON

In the days of Newton, before science began to get complicated, and the universe was a giant machine, there was no problem in understanding time. Time was linear. It had a beginning, a middle and an end. There was past, present and future. The most important facet of time was its uniformity. It was the one constant in nature. It always proceeded at the same speed.

This simplistic view of the universe was shattered by Einstein. The concept of time as constant had to be abandoned and henceforth space and time were indissolubly linked. Just as space was inconstant and subject to gravity, so was its temporal companion. According to Einstein, the upper limit of time's progress was the speed of light.

It is certainly helpful to view time and space as the same and thus to equate the two. If we look at the planets orbiting the Sun, we can see the same phenomenon as either space or time. Let us take the apparent passage of the Sun throughout the year, illustrated in Figure 4.1.

Starting the year at the Vernal Equinox, we can see the Sun

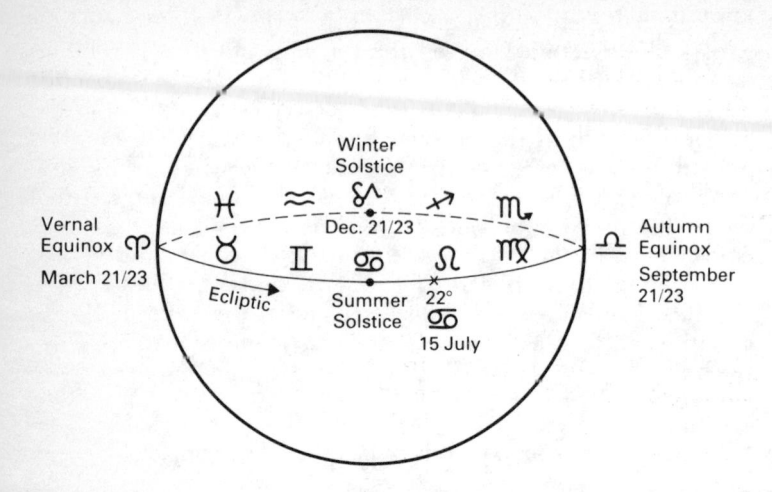

Figure 4.1 *The Sun's annual path through space and time as seen from the Earth*

moving from the beginning of Aries, taking approximately one day to travel along one degree of the ecliptic on its annual path around the Earth. We can also see this passage in another way. Instead of observing the Sun in terms of time, travelling one day through each degree of the ecliptic, we can see the same path as space. Then we see the Sun travelling through Aries into Taurus and so on round the Zodiac.

But the analogy between space and time can be carried too far. Space/time can reasonably be seen as a union, but in practice the way scientists conceive their model is to add time on to space as a fourth dimension. Now superficially this sounds attractive, but what is actually happening? In reality this is not a genuine four-dimensional model at all, and harm is done because on the surface it appears to be four-dimensional. In fact the way scientists conceive space/time is not as a true whole, but rather as time being added to the pre-existing concept of space as a linear phenomenon. So time, instead of forming a union with space, simply becomes a poor relation rather than an equal partner.

When we examine the model for what it really is, we find that instead of a four-dimensional model, we have a three-dimensional model of combined space/time which is a very different thing. What we need to do, is first to unite the concept of space/time into one. And then, and only then, add a new dimension, effectively a fifth dimension to the total picture. Only in this way will we see space/time as a unity.

In quantum physics scientists have come tantalizingly close to grasping this principle. On a superficial view the concept of the whole appears to be accepted. Then on closer examination it disappears. The reasons are twofold. On the one hand, although scientists, or some of the more progressive among them, are learning to see the whole as well as the parts, the relationship between them is not fully understood. The whole and the parts are effectively seen as separate, and thus the basic concept of separateness continues to underlie and undermine scientific understanding. On the other hand, for all their desire for unity, the assumptions of causality, which themselves are based on separation between the observed and the observer, remain.

Louis de Broglie has stated:

> In space-time, everything which for each of us constitutes the past, the present and the future is given en bloc.... Each observer, as his time passes, discovers so to speak, new slices of space-time which appear to him as successive aspects of the material world, though in reality the ensemble of events constituting space-time exist prior to his knowledge of them.[2]

Are we then any nearer to discovering the meaning of time? Are we helped by these scientific viewpoints? It seems to me that scientists have generally failed to understand the nature of time because they are confusing two systems. They can see that time appears to act as a measuring device, that it gets its entire meaning from events, that it only describes the relationship of various events with each other. That we therefore create time, just as we create space and matter, and that it is thus a mental construct. We do not perceive time itself, rather we perceive what goes on in time. And they can see that on one level, the sub-atomic, quantum level, time, like space and matter, is a whole. At the same time, when they actually look at it, they only see the parts. Although they talk of time as a unity, the language used is that of causality, of separation. And this surely is the fundamental misconception, as I have constantly pointed out in this book. The parts need to be seen in relationship to the whole. The parts exist. They are real on one level. The whole exists. It, too, is real on its level. And the one is contained in the other.

This is the paradox of time. It is one thing and it is another. One of the reasons scientists cannot see that is because they base their ideas on the materialist assumptions that were stated by Bertrand Russell – a thing cannot be and not be at the same time. I said when they 'actually look at time'. Here is the clue to the dilemma. It is the way scientists look at time that is wrong. To see time as it is, we must alter our perception, we must learn to see in a new way, a way which is effectively five-dimensional.

We can see the paradox when we look at some of the basic problems that are associated with time, both in science and Astrology. In Astrology, what we are looking at when we view the Horoscope is one moment of time describing time as a whole. That moment of time, the moment of birth, contains all time. And what we need to understand is the relationship between that one moment and all time.

'One moment' does not exist on its own. It is a mental construct, a symbol. Change is the physical reality; time a conceptual entity. We should see each part, each moment of time, the Horoscope, as part of the whole. For each part contains the whole. It is our individual window whence we view eternity. Eternity resides in the whole. We create time and space. How we choose to see the universe depends on us. We can see the parts or the whole. We can see time in the motion, in the photons of light. Or eternity in the stillness, the radiation, the infinite recurrence of the waves.

2 THE SYMBOLISM OF TIME

> The dance along the artery
> The circulation of the lymph
> Are figured in the drift of stars.
> T.S. Eliot

That there are two ways of seeing time should now be clear. The mystic, the poet and the artist, see time as unity, as being, or eternity. The scientist, and the materialist, see time as linear, separate, part of their dualistic view of the world. Unfortunately, the paucity of our language fails to distinguish between the two. The Greeks, however, called 'timeless time' or eternity Kairos, and mundane time Kronos.

Contrary to what may appear at first sight, the answer to time is not that there are two kinds of time, but that there are two ways of looking at time. And that both, Kairos and Kronos, co-exist. Each is contained in the other. Scientists cannot find the timeless quality of time, not because they do not see it, but because they fail to recognize it when they do see it.

The view of the mystic and the view of the scientist are each correct as far as they go. They each describe one aspect of time. But to find the meaning of time the two need to be combined. The answer we get depends on the question we ask. What do we ask of time? The scientist wants to know what time is. But he does not ask time its meaning. And so he cannot complain when he finds that time has no meaning.

But the opposite view, that time as we know it is not real, and that the only reality is eternity, is equally fraught with difficulties. This is particularly dangerous for the astrologer. For time is the astrologer's cornerstone. And this means time on a material as well as on a 'spiritual' level. The astrologer must of course be aware of the eternal, of the divine spark within him. This is reality at the spiritual level. But because the spiritual is real, it does not mean that the physical world we live in is unreal.

Insisting that only the spiritual or the material is real is equally misleading. It is, of course, difficult to reconcile the two, but this is the need for mankind at this time. And this is the very task that the astrologer needs to carry out in order to help mankind. Meister Eckhart has said: 'A master says: "He whose being and work is altogether in eternity, and he whose being and work is altogether in time, they are never in accord, they never come together." '[3] But the astrologer is not only a mystic, nor is he only a scientist. Astrology embraces both science and art as a symbolic system of understanding. In Astrology the two can and must come together.

Can we then reconcile the two? How can we be whole, how can we see in a way that embraces the eternal or divine and yet continue to live in a world that is temporal and material? The answer is first to appreciate that both the eternal and the temporal are contained within us. In order to see both, we need to be in touch with both levels that are already present in us.

To quote Meister Eckhart again: 'The soul is created as if at a point between time and eternity, which touches both. With the higher powers she touches eternity, but with the lower powers she touches time.'[4] If we seek the meaning of time then we shall find it in the symbolic nature of time. As Michael Shallis has written: 'The paradox of Astrology is a paradox resolved when all time is seen to be symbolic.'[5]

In symbolic, or mythological time, eternity and mundane time meet. 'Mythological time,' says Emma Brunner-Trant: 'is not scientific time and allows the timeless to shine through. It is their relationship to time that divides the mythically orientated and the historically minded man.... He who only measures and calculates finds no access to that which cannot be grasped by the space-time concept. For mythical understanding does not aim at the known order but regulates to that which in itself creates, contains and presents both question and answer.'[6]

When we stop to think about it, it is clear that there cannot be an objective difference between the two kinds of time. We can only live in the present. The difference arises in how we view this present. As T.S. Eliot has written:

> Time past and time future
> What might have been and what has been
> Point to one end, which is always present.

But we can, and do, view this present moment in two different ways. Indeed, in two opposing ways. We can either see the present as the only reality, as eternity, or alternatively, as unreal, as time. The world we see will never be the same, each moment is different, and yet the present is timeless.

One viewpoint is that we can only live in the present, in this moment of time, and therefore we are always living in this moment, in the present. Therefore the present is eternal. That is what eternity means. Living in the eternal present. Living for the moment and in the moment. This is the mystic way. This is what Meister Eckhart meant when he wrote: 'The Now in which God made the first man and the Now in which the last man shall cease to be, and the Now I speak in, all are the same in God and there is but one Now.'[7]

But it is equally valid to say that it is only the present which does not exist. Even while I think of this moment, it has passed. Inexorably it has become a part of my past. What I think of as the present is the future. I cannot grasp the present moment. It is no more than a convenient, and artificial, dividing line between the reality of past and future.

This is the materialist's viewpoint. For him there is only birth and death with life sandwiched between these two certainties. But it is just because we try to grasp the present moment, that it eludes us. Our whole lives become a desperate effort to use time, to be busy, to ensure that not a moment of precious time is lost. And it is precisely in this way that all time is lost. For it is the quality of time that matters. It is simply, and only, by being that we are inescapably in time, and of time.

In chapter 1, I recounted the mythological story of Anki, the mountain of Heaven and Earth. When the mountain was cut into two the world as we know it came into being. Then time became separated from eternity. But the two still remained contained in the mountain. If we are united, we can see both for both are contained in us.

This myth is an archetypal one which is common, with certain variations, in many cultures. In the Greek myth, subsequently taken over by the Romans, Gaia was the Earth mother who gave birth to Ouranos, the sky or Heaven. From the mating of mother and son came six male and six female children, corresponding to the twelve signs of the Zodiac.

The youngest male child was Kronos or Saturn who castrated Ouranos. Thus Time destroyed Eternity and ended the marriage of Heaven and Earth, and thus was the material world brought into being. Kronos is the god associated particularly with physical manifestation, and we have seen that he represented mundane time. He represents the boundaries of the physical world, and his cross is the cross of matter, which nails the spirit to the wheel of life through the four Angles of the Horoscope. He is the Earth; and Enlil, who in common with his Greek counterpart severed his parents, was also known as the Earth.

We have seen that materialistic cosmologies are based on a definite moment of creation. The esoteric branches of religion favour another view. While the Bible of the orthodox Old Testament describes God creating the world, the hidden doctrine of the Kabbalah conceives of creation as a gradual process of emanation from unmanifest to manifest. The Zohar compares creation to a silkworm spinning a cocoon out of itself. Out of the Void, which contains all potential within itself, the world as we know it gradually evolved from purity to grosser form until the material world came into being.

The same view is inherent in Islamic doctrine. From the Divine Essence (hadrat al-dhat) evolved the Presence of Divinity (hadrat al-uluhiyya), also known as the Universal Intellect (al-akl al kullig) corresponding to God being aware of Himself. Thence proceeded the Presence of the Masterhood (hadrat al-rububiyya) which contained the individual intelligences or agents of the Divine, those whom we know as the angels.

From this stage of existence was developed the Soul (barzakh), and finally the Physical World (Mushahada). Thence came the First Man (al-insan al-awwal) and then the rest of humanity and life.

These cosmologies contain the essential idea of the co-existence of eternity and time, the unity of the timeless with time. Each is contained in the other. Physical time cannot be banished from our physical world. Yesterday is past, today differs from tomorrow and each time has its peculiar quality. But equally, the world is, was and always will be and this unity can be glimpsed through each separate moment of time because it is contained in each moment of time. This is the important point. Eternity is contained, and therefore can be seen, in each separate moment. Time is thus the observation of eternity.

'I know that whatsoever God doeth, it will be for ever. That which has been is now, and that which is to be hath already been; and God requireth that which is past.'[8] Such is the mystic realization of oneness which, once experienced, can never be taken away. 'And there shall be no more death, neither sorrow, nor crying, neither shall there be any more pain: for the former things are passed away.'[9] We can choose our viewpoint. We can unite ourselves to the being, the wholeness of time and find there its meaning, or we can merely watch it glide past carrying us with it down the stream to an inevitable death.

In the religion of Mithra, which almost became the accepted religion of the Roman Empire instead of Christianity, the two kinds of time were united. Mitravarunan was both Varuna, the lord of cosmic rhythm, and Mitra, he who brings forth the light of dawn. Zervan Akarana was 'boundless time' — eternity and time in one. The Sun and Moon were a pair, not two separate entities. They represented the syzygy, the union of opposites, like the Nasatya or Ashvins, the twin horsemen.

The Sun was the Lion. It represented the eternal solar light. Never changing, fixed. The Moon was the serpent, the ouroboros which devoured its own tail. It symbolized the rhythmic, circling round of ceaseless time. Its phases changed constantly from night to night, sometimes vanishing altogether, sometimes shining in full glory like the Sun, always different yet always the same.

The Horoscope graphically illustrates both kinds of time. It contains the fixed dot at the centre. The still centre of Eternity around which the ceaseless circle of time revolves from everlasting to everlasting. We are both. While we inhabit this earth, we must tread the circumference of the ecliptic around which are placed the planets, the Signs and the Houses. But we are also at the centre when we are in touch with our inner selves. When we unite the two then being and doing are the same and we find the meaning of time and of life.

3 TIME'S WHEEL

Time's wheel runs back or stops: potter and clay endure.
Robert Browning

In general Astrology is concerned with the meaning of time. In particular, it is concerned with the quality of time. Jung made the point succinctly: 'Whatever is born or done this moment of time has the qualities of this moment of time.' Each moment of time represents the pattern, and the quality that is incorporated in that pattern, at the particular moment of time.

That is why one moment differs from another. But at the same time each moment incorporates the whole of time. Each moment of time incorporates the future as well as the present. As we shall see in the next chapter, the art of prediction is to see the future in the present.

The moment of birth encapsulates in its pattern a picture of the future of the person or event symbolized in the Horoscope. What we think of as past, present and future is, in reality, a unity. It is not a divided succession of sequences but a continuum.

This is something which is more readily expressed, because it is more immediately experienced, by the artist, whatever his medium. For the aim of the artist is to express the timeless, something which is eternal, a state of being, in a tangible form, whether it be words, paint or musical notation. The form, symbolized by Saturn or Kronos, places the subjective experience which is outside time, in time.

The point has been made by the composer, Norman Kay:

> I'm always struck by the fact that musical delight is bound up (for me) with the feeling that a great composer has mastered time. Not only that: he has reconciled two kinds of time – one the external area (let's say objective time), the other an individual (let's say psychological) time. The first is normally fixed, and it holds me in bondage; the second is more bound up with internal perceptions and fluctuations.[10]

The physicist is concerned with time as part of physical reality. The mystic is concerned with the subjective experience of time. The artist needs to translate this subjective experience into time, into an ordered structure so that he can communicate his inner experience symbolically to others. The astrologer, too, needs to experience eternity, the whole, through the individual moment of time. He needs to see the whole symbolically in the separate parts. Just as the words of the poet, and the musical notation of the composer, are a bridge between inner and outer, so is the moment of time of the Horoscope a bridge between two kinds of time.

To see the whole of reality we need to include subjective experience. Science, too, is finally realizing that there is no essential difference between what was believed to be 'out there' and what is 'in here'. The observer is an integral part of the world he observes. The real world includes us. It is a relationship between what we observe and ourselves. It is a union of two levels in us.

We can see matter divided up into separate parts. There are trees and stones and you and me. That is one level. We can also see, or experience, beneath this level. Here matter ceases to exist. There is only the field. Everything is a part of everything else, a continuum.

Time too exists on both levels. Each moment has a significance of its own. And each moment of time reaches out throughout the universe connecting all things. 'A moment of time is then like a virtual particle, appearing out of the vacuum of time and space yet interconnected with the whole universe.'[11]

The scientist and the mystic see time in different ways. The former sees a temporal world bounded by linear time and space. The latter sees eternity. Both are the same. The only difference is in the level or viewpoint. Eternity is incorporated in time. It is not something separate. It is simply seeing time in a different way.

Although we normally see time as moving, just as we see the planets and the hands of a clock moving, we sometimes seem to move into another sphere of time. Most people have had the experience, at some time in their lives, of being transported into another dimension of time, although few have appreciated the reality behind their experience.

Then we see as a whole, 'face to face' as St Paul said. Eternity is being. We are eternal when we are. It is difficult to see the same thing in two different ways at the same time. And it is difficult to get out of habits that have been ingrained over long periods of time. That is why self-realization often needs the shock of a sudden experience, like the blindness of St Paul, to shift one's level, and to enable us to see in this new way.

This is how we need to see the Horoscope, if we are to experience it for what it is. The whole universe is the outer manifestation of a moment of time. The universe is eternal. It is an endless pattern, a dance, continual motion. It is only when we observe it, that it becomes time. Plato wrote in the *Timaeus*: 'Wherefore he resolved to have a moving image of eternity, and when he set in order the heaven, he made this image eternal but moving according to number, while eternity itself results in unity; and this image we call Time.' In kabbalistic terms, we can see Eternity as force or Chokmah, the number 2, while Time corresponds to form, Binah or the number 3.

This brings us to an examination of the basis of the connection between the planetary movements and events on earth with particular reference to time. Specifically to an examination of causation and synchronicity.

The concept of synchronicity was one which Jung developed in order to try to explain the connection between events that appeared to have no causal relationship. He recounts how on one occasion a patient whom he was treating for a psychological disorder, complained of a sore throat. Jung advised the patient to see his doctor and, unknown to Jung, the patient collapsed from a heart attack and died on the way to the doctor.

The wife of the patient then called on Jung and asked if there was anything seriously wrong with her husband. On the face of it there was no reason for the patient's wife to be alarmed about her husband's physical condition when he was consulting Jung for a purely psychological problem, even if she was aware of his sore throat.

Jung therefore asked her why she was so concerned and was told that a flock of birds had arrived at her husband's bedroom window. In itself this occurrence would hardly be remarkable, but when this lady's grandfather lay dying a flock of birds had also appeared at his bedroom window, and the same phenomenon occurred when her father died.

It was clear to Jung that there was no causal connection between these deaths and the arrival of the flocks of birds. Certainly it was beyond belief that the birds caused these people to die. Whether in some way the approach of death could have caused the simultaneous approach of the birds is another question, but it is not one that could be answered affirmatively on the basis of current scientific knowledge at the time.

There was a coincidence here, and a coincidence which appeared to be meaningful. However, and this is the important point in this context, the coincidence was related by time. Life is full of coincidences. Most of them go unrecognized partly because they are of no great importance, and partly because we lack the awareness to give meaning to them. The point lies in recognizing the meaning in the coincidence and to appreciate the significance of time as a factor in the coincidence.

There is a pattern in time as well as in space. Each moment connects the whole universe, every living entity, every event. It is this pattern that is reflected in the pattern made by the planets in the sky. Each moment has its own meaning, its own significance. Time as well as space can be haunted. Colin Wilson has pointed out that attempts were made on the lives of both Rasputin and the Archduke Ferdinand at exactly the same time – 2.15 p.m. on 27 June 1914.

There are two points here. First, the element of time, sometimes involving the connection between two levels of time. And second, the meaning, which entails a connection between the outer phenomena and inner experience. Jean Bolen has written: 'Synchronicity is like a waking dream in which we experience the intersection of the timeless with time, where the impossible union of spheres of existence is actual, and where what is inside of us and what is outside is unseparated.'[12]

Synchronicity is quite common, for what is inside and what is outside are the same. Therefore the outer constantly and inevitably mirrors the inner. But if we do not recognize the symbolic meaning of the coincidence then we fail to see the occurrence as an example of synchronicity.

Synchronicity either connects two events at the same time, as happened in the case of Jung's patient. Here the coincidence of the birds and death was simultaneous. Other examples occur when we think of someone and at that precise moment that person telephones, or when someone has a dream or vision of an event which is taking place elsewhere at that time.

Alternatively, two different levels of time meet. Then there is a connection between one moment and the continuum of time. This occurs when a person has a premonition of an event that happens in the future.

The universe as we see it is the outer manifestation of a moment of time. It is reflected in every phenomenon. The I Ching says: 'As the moment is, so do the runic sticks fall.' That moment is reflected in the planetary motions, the pattern in an animal's liver, the fall of the jarrow sticks.

To understand the connection between eternity and time, inner and outer, we need to be aware of the three levels that we examined in chapter 3: the spiritual, the astral and the physical.[13] The eternal, spiritual, level has been described in the T'an Ching:

> In this moment, there is nothing which comes to be. In this moment there is nothing which ceases to be. Thus there is no birth-and-death to be brought to an end. Wherefore the absolute tranquility (of nirvana) is this present moment. Though it is at this moment that there is no limit to this moment, and herein is eternal delight.

How then do we reach this state? How do we get in touch with the Eternal? The difficulty has been stated by Meister Eckhart: 'There is no greater obstacle to Union with God than Time.'[14] And in another way by Krishna to Arjuna: 'I know, O Arjuna! all things in the past, the present and the future; but they do not know Me.'

The intersection between the timeless and time occurs between the spiritual and the physical levels. On the level which can be termed the astral or the unconscious. That is why we need to be aware of the unconscious if we are to be open to experience and meaning. 'For synchronicity to happen,' writes Jean Bolen, 'the space between individuals and things, rather than being empty, must somehow "contain" a connecting link or be a transmission medium. Jung calls this the collective unconscious.'[15] Occultists call it the astral plane.

If we recognize the relationship between inner and outer, and the relationship between the moment and time as a whole, we shall understand the meaning in what occurs in the world. We can if we choose, see the same thing as synchronicity or causation. We can say that the flock of birds is drawn to the person who is about to die, and so he causes their arrival. Or we can simply recognize the meaning between the birds and the person's death.

We looked at the E–R–P experiment in chapter 2. When one particle changed its direction its partner did likewise. The physicists, with their causal assumptions, were driven to look for a physical signal between the two particles. And problems arose when one particle was light years away from the other, for according to the laws of classical physics nothing could exceed the speed of light and thus the signal would be sent after it had been received, reversing the arrow of time.

In one sense it does not matter whether one sees a phenomenon as synchronicity or causation. If we accept the thesis that there is only the whole and that we see the whole on our physical plane through the parts then both are the same. The connection between outer and inner is symbolized in what happens on the physical level. What matters is to recognize the meaning behind the level.

These levels exist in all of us. We can experience any state in one of three ways. We can see the same phenomenon as linear time or as eternity or as the intersection of the timeless and time. If we are to be whole people we need to experience time on all levels. On the spiritual level, time is irrelevant. But on the physical level, it is vital. It is the factor above all which, rightly understood, gives meaning to astrological theory.

4 THE RIGHT TIME

In learning to appreciate the higher levels, we can succumb to the temptation of devaluing the material level. Either extreme is as dangerous as the other. The danger of devaluing mundane time is that we fail to understand the importance of the right time. The physical world is based on mundane time. Each time has its individual quality just as each person born, and each thing done, has the quality of that time. The key to understanding physical manifestation through Astrology lies in understanding the way that time differs, just as the key to understanding spiritual reality lies in understanding the way that time is united.

There is a right time for everything. A right time and a wrong time. This does not mean that we should try to manipulate time. On the contrary, it means living in accordance with the quality of the time. It is a useful exercise to see the universe simply as time. To imagine oneself simply as an event moving through time, without a body, in a spaceless universe.

The different qualities of time are apparent, to some extent at least, to everyone. We all know the difference between the seasons. The most unappreciative city-dweller looks forward to the spring after the rigours of winter. Even he can acknowledge the freshness of the morning, the heaviness of noon and the tranquillity of the evening.

What are not so apparent are the greater cycles of time which embrace generations, centuries, millenia. These periods too vary in quality. Each is like a wave, having its peaks and troughs.

Nowhere is the principle put more dramatically than in the famous passage from Ecclesiastes which is worth quoting in full:

> To every thing there is a season, and a time to every purpose under the heaven:
> A time to be born, and a time to die; a time to plant, and a time to pluck up that which is planted;
> A time to kill, and a time to heal; a time to break down, and a time to build up;
> A time to weep, and a time to laugh; a time to mourn, and a time to dance;
> A time to cast away stones, and a time to gather stones together; a time to embrace, and a time to refrain from embracing;
> A time to get, and a time to lose; a time to keep, and a time to cast away;
> A time to rend, and a time to sew; a time to keep silence, and a time to speak;
> A time to love, and a time to hate; a time of war, and a time of peace.[16]

We can see the reflections of these times when we look at the births of people and of events. Why famous people are born at certain times, and equally why certain people are famous. They are the children of their time. They were born at the right time. Thales, Confucius, the Buddha, Zoroaster, four of the greatest religious men from four corners of the earth, were all born around 600 B.C.. J.S. Bach and Handel were born within days of each other. Newton and Leibnitz invented the calculus at the same time. John Couch Adams and Urbaine Leverrier discovered Neptune simultaneously.

Shakespeare wrote: 'There are many events in the womb of time which will be delivered.' But only at the right time. In chapter 2, I described the momentous discovery by Madam Wu in 1956 that parity is not conserved. That crucial experiment had already been carried out by C.T. Chase. He observed asymmetry, distinguishing left from right, in an experiment exactly the same as that carried out by Madam Wu. The only difference was that Chase carried out his experiment in 1930. It was dismissed with the verdict 'error due to causes unknown'. The time was not then right.

Why was Hitler great? It might convincingly be argued that in himself he was nothing. The archetypal little man, with few talents. Tragically the time was right for him. His personal vision coincided with the time in which he was born. Jesus too was born at the right time. For years the Messiah had been prophesied. Many Messiahs had come and gone. Sunk into oblivion with no trace. Then, under the first great conjunction of Saturn and Jupiter in Pisces, heralding the Great Age of Pisces, the Christ was born at Bethlehem. And at his crucifixion he said: 'My time is at hand.'[17]

The cycles of time are the measurement of change; they are necessary for the purpose of the universe to be realized. Although at the higher level, the world simply is, at the mundane level it is ceaseless change. It is a dance of endless energy. In its entirety it is the Tao. And at one level it is unity, containing all opposites. At another, it is the I Ching, the book of changes.

Each moment of time has a different resonance, a different harmony, a different quality. In each moment, the various cycles inter-relate. The millenia, the centuries, the years, the months, the days, the hours will converge and meet at a particular moment in time. Within each moment is contained the multitudes of the different cycles. Each is a part of the whole, inextricably joined together.

These various cycles, of course, coincide with the cycles of the planets and the earth itself. Each cycle, each factor of time in the Cosmos, has its tides and seasons of ascendancy. It is the knowledge of these cycles that is used in choosing the time for a magical or religious ceremony, and in Electional Astrology, which is specifically concerned with choosing the correct time for a particular event.

The tides of the year are mirrored in those of the day. Figure 4.2 illustrates the correlation. Both the year and the day are divided in two ways. First, in the Cardinal points. In the year, at the equinoxes and solstices. These correspond in the diurnal cycle to dawn and dusk, midday and midnight. The equinoxes are times of change. Days and nights are equal at the beginning of Aries and Libra and then they get longer and shorter respectively. Dawn and dusk, too, are times of change and one can feel the stillness that precedes these times.

The solstices are times of fullness. The longest day at the beginning of Cancer and the longest night at the beginning of Capricorn, corresponding to midday and midnight. At each of these turning points of the year and day one of the Elements is in its ascendancy and so the four points are ruled by the four archangels of the Elements. Raphael, the archangel of Air, ruling the dawn and spring; Michael, archangel of Fire, ruling noon and summer; Gabriel, archangel of Water, ruling the evening and autumn; and Uriel, archangel of Earth, holding sway over midnight and winter.

These divisions represent beginnings. The flow of a new kind of energy. The second division represents the accumulated force of power which is concentrated in the middle of the Fixed Signs. These points are known as 'power points' and this is where the great forces are concentrated during the year, and to a lesser extent, during the day. So we have change and fixity alternating throughout the two periods.

The importance of appreciating the qualities of these times, is not just for the practical purposes of choosing the right day and time for a particular activity, but to ensure that we do what it is in our nature to do at the right time. Thus we align inner and outer. Like the seagull gliding through the air, using the

THE MYSTERY OF TIME

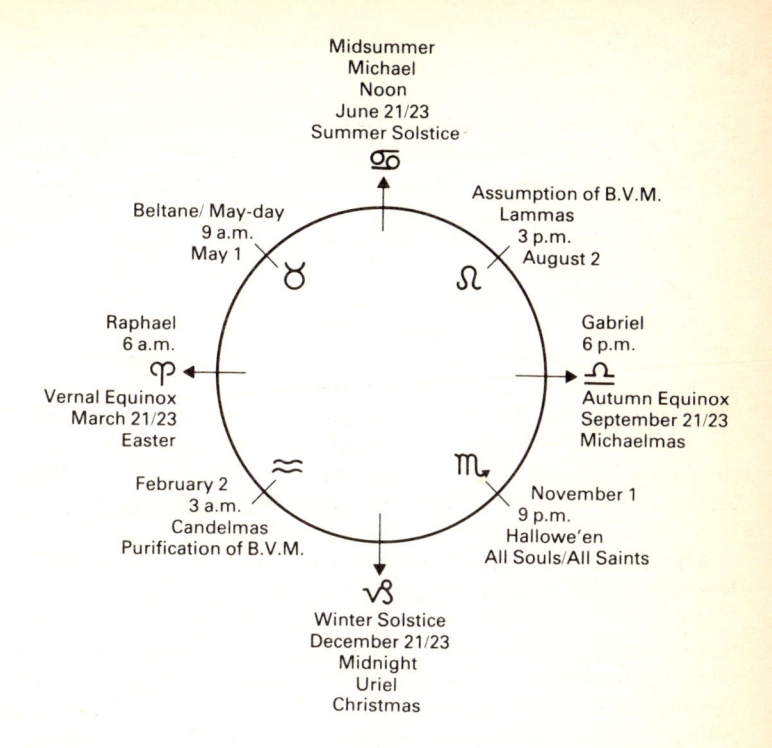

Figure 4.2 *The correlation of the tides of the year and the day*

currents of the wind, conserving its energy and flowing with nature, we become an integral part of the universe.

Each of us is his or her time. Each represents a particular time. Each individual is unique and special in his or her own way. Each of us is created for a particular purpose. Each has been given a specific psychological anatomy which is tuned into the celestial pattern of the universe at the moment of our birth.

There is a kabbalist tradition that we are held in the Treasure House of Souls until it is time for us to be incarnated into a physical body. When the situation arises that suits the needs of our spirit's particular purpose, then at the moment of birth, the soul's psychological body is set according to the state of the macrocosmic world at that moment.

For our ancestors the word Horoscope had a different meaning to the one we have given it. For them it was not just the moment of birth, but the *right* moment to be born. The word 'hora' meant the 'correct moment', and was derived from the three Horai, the daughters of Themis, who represented the law of nature. The Horai were Eunomia, lawful order, Dike, just retribution or Nemesis, and Eirene, peace. These three were entrusted with the guardianship of the gates of Heaven. It is in the principle of Dike in particular that we can see the meaning of the Horoscope as the ancients conceived it. Hers was the axiom of Justice in accordance with nature. Not punishment, as we tend to think of Nemesis today, but the inevitable reaction inherent in nature as when the hand is burnt if it is put into the fire.

It was the principle of putting right what was out of place. The aim was equilibrium, a redress of the balance symbolized by the scales of justice. If a person did not live in accordance with his Horoscope, he would invoke the force of this law. That was Nemesis. The point, therefore, was to balance one's energies, to live in accordance with the whole of one's Horoscope.

And originally the word 'Horoskopos' meant only the ascendant point or degree. It was the fixed star or planet which was 'born' into the sky at the same moment as the child was born. Hence came the belief that everyone was born under his own star and that the child's star contained his guardian angel or spirit who would protect him.

This then, the time of our birth, is our time. We should not, and need not, be concerned about the time we are born. The time we are born is the time we should have been born. We should not, and need not, try to manipulate nature. We need only be the people we already are. We need only be a part of the nature whose essence we contain. There are times for princes to be born, and times for priests and for poets. If we understand the cycles of time we shall be helped to a greater understanding of the meaning of our particular lives, of our unique purpose in this incarnation. Then we can echo the words of Pope John XXIII: 'Any day is a good day to be born, and any day is a good day to die.'

5 THE UNION OF TIME

It is in the Horoscope that time is united. Here eternity and time, Kairos and Kronos, meet. This is the intersection between the timeless and time. The Horoscope is symbolic of both kinds of time. The eternal, unceasing circle, the snake eating its own tail from everlasting to everlasting, is fixed in the cross of matter, the four Elements which make up the physical world, and the two axes – vertical and horizontal – that are contained within the totality of the Self.

While the concepts of Astrology were being formulated, it was a matter of controversy whether Astrology was a time or a space system. Time cannot be separated from space but a great deal of confusion has arisen because the two have been mixed without appreciating the underlying significance of each.

It is clear that the Birth Chart represents a moment of time. It is also clear that the pattern of the planets at that particular moment is a picture of the spatial position of those planets in particular areas of the sky. We have already seen how the planetary positions can be seen either as their route through space or through time. In Figure 4.1 the position of the Sun can be seen as either 22 degrees of Cancer or as 15 July.

The Babylonians felt space to be of prime importance. They were concerned at the outset with the physical appearance and spatial position of the planets, and in particular with the Moon. If an eclipse was not visible at any specific location, then it had no effect at that place.

If Venus shone brightly in a particular area of the sky then its effect would be felt by whatever came under the rulership of that area. If Mars was in Capricorn then its influence would extend to everything over which Capricorn exercised dominion. The Moon afflicted in Aries would cause fires and strife.

The Egyptians, on the other hand, laid stress on a planet being at a certain time rather than at a point in space. For them the Zodiac was the Sun's journey through the year. It was the time that the Sun took to travel round the Earth. Each point on this journey, each portion of time, was guarded by its own god or spirit, by its protecting genius.

Thus for the Egyptians, Astrology was primarily a time system. And this viewpoint was taken over by the Greeks. The gods or guardian spirits who ruled over and protected each day and hence each degree of the Zodiac, were called the Monomorai. The thirty-six gods who controlled the dekans were the Daimons.

As Stobaios put it:

> Nothing ... occurs without the influence of the dekans. And ... as the dekans have command over the planets and as we are under the dominion of the Seven, don't you see that a certain influence from the dekans reaches down as far as us.[18]

The distinction between space and time is of importance when it comes to understanding how different cultures have viewed astrological principles. If space is of prime importance, then what matters is that a planet or other factor is in a certain Sign of the Zodiac and a certain House in the diurnal system. Similarly the physical distance between the planets will be of major significance.

Naturally this view is more prevalent among cultures which are concerned in particular with material phenomena, as in western cultures. Therefore the Signs, Houses and aspects between the planets will be regarded as important in themselves. The Moon in Figure 1.1 takes on its distinguishing characteristics because it is in the Sign of Taurus, in the 10th House, and makes a square aspect to Jupiter and a sextile aspect to the Sun and Venus.

Looked at in this way, and this is the traditional way of looking at the phenomena of Astrology, the area in the sky known as Taurus has a particular quality of its own quite different from the adjacent one known as Gemini. Similarly, the area in the diurnal circle called the 10th House has its own meaning which differs from its neighbour, the 11th House. Difficulties naturally arise in this viewpoint as the Signs differ according to different systems.

Owing to the precession of the equinoxes there is now a

difference of approximately twenty-four degrees between the Signs in the Tropical and the Sidereal Zodiacs. So most of the factors which are in one Sign according to the Tropical Zodiac, will be in the neighbouring Sign according to the Sidereal Zodiac, and vice versa. The differences between the Houses is even more acute with the vast number of different systems in current use, putting the planets not just in adjacent Houses but sometimes even further away.

If, however, one regards Astrology primarily as a time system, then one does not see the Signs in themselves as of importance. Then the forces of the Zodiac are not so much emanations to Earth of the constellations themselves, but rather they are seen as markers on a great clock which indicates the type of energy emanating from the Sun at any particular time.

So the Zodiac is regarded as the Sun's journey in time around the Earth, viewed from our terrestrial standpoint. It represents 'zones' or 'rays' of influence which touch the Earth at certain seasons. The area of the sky we call Taurus has no identity in itself. It merely represents the portion of the sky along which the Sun travels at a certain time of the year.

The Moon's position in this area of the sky is only significant according to this view because it partakes of the solar influence when it travels through that portion of the ecliptic. Clearly, in this view, it is the Sun alone which is the important factor as it is its journey which is reflected by the other factors in their passage along its path.

Which of these viewpoints then is correct? Should we regard the Signs of the Zodiac as meaningful in themselves or should we look only at the planets in relation to each other? This question is of practical importance for astrologers today and it threatens to divide practitioners in their work.

As a practical question, it is both valid and necessary to bear both views in mind. If one treats the two viewpoints separately, as one is perfectly entitled to do, then one can see obvious merits in both. Just as one can see obvious merits in regarding light both as a particle and as a wave phenomenon. We have seen from the experiments that have been carried out that light must be a particle phenomenon because waves can only travel through something, and it has been proved that the 'ether' does not exist. But similarly light must be a wave phenomenon to account for its dispersal through the two-slit experiment.

The differences in the Signs can be seen on the most mundane level by anyone who is at all aware of their intrinsic nature. They can be seen in the physical divergence in a person with a Taurean as opposed to a Geminian Ascendant as much as in the quality of a day when the Moon is in one of those two Signs. Equally, it should be apparent from what we have already said in this chapter that a Birth Chart is literally a particular moment in time, and a person born at one time is different from his fellow born at another time even though the individual factors in both charts are almost identical.

Before we look at time and space in more detail, it is important from the philosophical viewpoint to try to see the essential principle behind both time and space. In looking only at the differences, it is easy to fall into the trap of seeing only the effects rather than seeking the unity behind the manifest duality.

Space and time are the same thing on different levels. Space is form; it is the state of mundane existence and corresponds with the number 3. Time is the force behind the form, the pattern behind the shape and corresponds with the number 2. Each moment in time is a pattern in space. The Horoscope combines the two. It is a moment in time and it is graphically represented as a spatial picture of the planetary positions. The reality lies in the symbol, or more accurately, in the truth behind the symbol.

Everything in the universe which is born in that moment of time is that pattern. This is what connects time and space. The planets move in their spheres in space and every moment produces a new pattern, a new vibration. Whether we see that moment as time or space depends upon our frame of reference. The answer depends upon the question. Reality is contained in both, and the essence of both is contained in their unity.

Until now, we have talked about a 'moment of time'. We have described the Horoscope as a 'moment of time'. But before we look at time more carefully from the point of view of prediction in the next chapter, we need to ask ourselves just what we mean by this term. What is a 'moment of time'? Into what division does this term fall? A day, an hour, a minute, a second? To ask this question is not to be pedantic. It is vital to our understanding of time that we appreciate the basic fact that there is no such thing as a 'moment of time'.

The division of the Zodiac into dekans and degrees reveals a difficulty that tends to be glossed over. Any division, whether of time or space, is a matter of convenience. Just as there are no lines in nature but we make them up in order to contain what we see, so we divide time up so that we can think about it.

The artist knows that his lines are artificial. They give form to the underlying content. They are a part of his art. It is easy for someone who is not an artist to forget this basic fact, or fail to realize it in the first place. Similarly, we should remember that time as a measuring device is an artificial mental construct, and as such it is useful only so long as the reality behind it is appreciated.

No harm is done provided we realize the artificiality of our terminology. It is useful and necessary to use these divisions just as it is useful and necessary to use lines in art. The astronomer has broken down his division of a second into a 919,263,1770th part for greater accuracy. Perhaps each of these divisions has its guardian spirit. Perhaps this is currently the number of angels that could stand on the head of a pin.

What we need always to appreciate is that this division is a result of the duality of our minds. Therefore, at the physical level, this is how we see nature. But we also need to see the total pattern behind the division. Then we see with our spiritual nature, or strictly speaking, with the Higher Mind. Then we see as a whole.

By thinking of a moment of time we make the wheel stop. It is like looking at a single shot in a reel of film. We need to do this to see that particular shot with all its details clearly. But the danger of mistaking the convenience for the reality is that we forget that the wheel never stops moving, that what we are looking at is part of the motion, a piece of the tail that is being swallowed.

Both kinds of time, Kairos and Kronos, are contained and combined in the Horoscope. The Horoscope is the intersection of the two in what we, for convenience, call a 'moment of time'. Kairos exists now and forever. It is a state. As we shall see in the next chapter, the art of prediction lies in the ability to get in touch with this state.

CHAPTER 5
A view of the future – prediction and free will

> Ye shall know the truth and the truth shall make you free.
> John 8.32

Are we free? This question has been asked by philosophers ever since they had the freedom to think. It is a question of vital importance to astrologers. It is the question we shall now consider. But we need to be careful that we ask this question without making preconceived assumptions, which themselves limit our freedom.

It is easy to be emotional about freedom. We begin with the premise that we must have freedom, or worse still, that we must have possessed freedom originally. Or we beg the very question, like Jean-Jacques Rousseau in his classic statement: 'L'homme est né libre, et partout il est dans les fers.'

These preconceived assumptions may be of no great matter for scientists and philosophers. But the question of free will is of vital importance for the astrologer because part of his art consists of foretelling the future. There are some who are so confused by the whole question that they turn their backs on the issue and refuse to have anything to do with prediction. But pretending that something does not exist does not help to understand it.

Whether the astrologer likes it or not, prediction is an integral aspect of his art. As such it is the duty of every astrologer to come to a proper understanding of this subject, whether or not he predicts himself. That the future is an integral part of the present is inherent in the Birth Chart itself.

At the very moment of birth, simply by looking at a child's Horoscope, and without examining the future contacts that the planets will make to it, the astrologer can tell, or foretell, the relationship between the child and his parents, the way he is most likely to react to the situations which will occur in his life, and his attitude, and this inevitably means his future attitude, towards other people.

Thus there is no getting away from the future. Of course, the implications contained in the Birth Chart do not necessarily mean that the future can be foretold exactly. But that the future is in some way contained in the present is implicit in the Horoscope itself. What we want to know is why and how the future is encapsulated in the present moment.

The trouble with most astrologers in practice is that they know perfectly well that they can see the future contacts the planets will make. They can predict exactly when each factor in a Birth Chart will be activated by a planet in the sky using one of the many predictive techniques. But at the same time they, quite naturally, do not want to rob people of their freedom of choice, so they try to compromise by taking up a meaningless half-way attitude. They say they can predict general trends but not specific events.

Like party political promises this may sound convincing to those who are incapable of, or unwilling to, think the problems through. But what does it really mean? Free will implies being able to change the future. Prediction implies the ability to tell what will happen in the future, which in turn implies the proposition that the future exists at the time it is being foretold, in other words, in the present.

If the future and the present co-exist, if the whole of time is a unity, then it is simply a question of getting in touch with something which is already in existence. That is what appears to happen in time travel, in dreams and premonitions. We then get a glimpse of the future. There is no point in trying to evade the issue by vague talk of trends. If we are to be open we need to examine the evidence in a truly scientific fashion, otherwise we cannot hope to arrive at the right answers.

1 THE SEEDS OF TIME – FREEDOM IN THE PHYSICAL WORLD

> If you can look into the seeds of time,
> And say which grain will grow and which will not.
> SHAKESPEARE, 'Macbeth'

Before the physical world, or rather scientists' concepts of the physical world, were upset by the quantum revolution and the fall of parity, the underlying aim of science was to find laws which enabled scientists to predict the results of their experiments.

The scientist had only to learn as much as possible about these laws and, as Laplace postulated, if there was a mind that knew all the existing facts, it would be possible to predict the future exactly. According to this viewpoint effect inevitably followed cause. There was no room for freedom here. The universe was a giant clockwork which had been wound up at the moment of creation and which would run in its predetermined way until its inevitable end.

Now, however, this view of the universe has changed. At the quantum level events cannot be predicted. This is for two reasons. First, because phenomena cannot be observed without the observer altering the results of the experiment. Second, because as we have seen in the E–R–P paradox, sub-atomic particles appear to change their paths according to the movements of each other. So at this level, matter appears to be conscious.

At the material level there is structure and pattern which enables us to say that, as a matter of probability, a particular phenomenon will occur in the future or be found in a certain place. Ephemerides of the planetary positions are published giving the exact position of the planets for years to come, railway time-tables are printed on the basis of future expectations.

Meteorologists tell us what weather we can expect in the future, actuaries tell us when we can expect to die. The degree of accuracy in these forecasts naturally varies. It has indeed always been a source of philosophic speculation as to whether anything can really be predicted as a matter of certainty. For predictions at this level are made on the basis of what has happened in the past. We say that the Sun will rise tomorrow because it has risen without fail for millions of years. Tomorrow it may explode. And indeed, if anything is certain, it is that one day the Sun will not rise.

Predictions about the rising of the Sun and the planetary positions are made on the basis of past evidence. Predictions about the weather and the time of death are made on the basis of statistics. In both cases it can only be said that an event will occur as a matter of probability.

But there is a vital difference in the subject-matter to which the probability relates. In the case of the Sun rising or a planet occupying a certain area of the ecliptic at a certain time, we can say without doubt that it will be the Sun in our solar system and Uranus in our solar system which will rise or be found at twenty-two degrees of Sagittarius on 26 February 1986, providing certain eventualities do not occur, like the universe coming to an end in the meantime.

However, in the case of statistics we are not concerned with the individual at all. Actuaries can say that the most likely time of death for someone who smokes fifty cigarettes a day is fifty-eight, but Mrs Jones may survive until she is ninety-five, while Mr Smith dies at thirty-two.

At the sub-atomic level predictions are made on this statistical basis. The sub-atomic scientist knows nothing about the individual particle. He cannot see it, or measure it or weigh it. He makes his predictions solely on the basis of averages. He can say that half the number of particles are likely to act in a certain way, and the other half are likely to act in another way. But he can never say how any individual particle will act.

This is a point which is of vital significance for astrologers, particularly as the role of statistics is increasing. It should never be forgotten when we look at the statistics of those like Michel Gauquelin showing that 27.8 per cent of sports champions are likely to have their Mars at the end of the 12th House,[1] that this figure does not tell us where any particular sports champion will have his Mars, or even whether any individual sports champion had his Mars in this area of the Birth Chart.

The situation can be misleading for the statistics will be true even though not one single sports champion has his Mars in this 'peak' position. It is like saying that the most common number of children for families today is 2.4, which of course is the one number which no family has.

What is valid for the scientist is not valid for the astrologer. The astrologer is concerned with the individual sports champion. The fact that 27.8 per cent of sports champions are likely to have their Mars in a certain position is simply an average and as such bears no relation to reality. As Bertrand Russell has said: 'Statistics, ideally, are accurate laws about large groups; they differ from other laws in being about groups, not about individuals.'

The fall of parity also meant that it was impossible to predict which end the particles would emerge – north or south. The universe is no longer made up of fixed, determined laws. As we have seen the degree of asymmetry involved here was slight. It has only been found in the weak force. But the point is whether there is freedom in the physical world, or whether there is not. That is the principle. If there is freedom then the principle is established. If there is not, then we need seek no further in the physical world.

What the discovery of asymmetry on the physical level means in philosophic terms is that material existence is not perfect. It is, therefore, no longer possible to foretell the future simply by knowing the past, no matter how inclusive our knowledge of the past may be. In the words of Feynman: 'God made the laws only nearly symmetrical so that we should not be jealous of His perfection.'

2 FREEDOM AND TIME

> ... Only by the form
> Can words or music reach
> The stillness, as a Chinese jar still
> Moves perpetually in its stillness.
> Not the stillness of the violin, while the note lasts,
> Not that only, but the co-existence,
> Or say that the end precedes the beginning,
> And the end and the beginning were always there
> Before the beginning and after the end.
> And all is always now.
>   T.S. ELIOT, 'Burnt Norton'

What are we actually looking at when we see the future? This is a question so fundamental that it is usually overlooked. There is no doubt that people do at times see the future. And if all time is a unity, if past, present and future co-exist, then we can have no control over the future.

Thus we are faced with a dilemma. If time, like space, simply is, if the future exists in the present, if time, as in T.S. Eliot's simile, is like a Chinese jar, where the whole jar exists and we, like flies, crawl around the outside, then we can only move along a predetermined path.

According to this view we cannot see the future, not because it does not exist, but because we are living in a three-dimensional state. With four-dimensional powers we could see the whole jar, we could watch our inevitable paths just as we could see the future path of a train from our vantage point on a bridge, but not if we were travelling inside the train.

There are many recorded cases of people seeing something that occurs in the future. They see an aircrash which subsequently occurs. Other, less dramatic cases are shrugged off. On one occasion my wife mentioned the announcement of someone's death on the television news. I looked for details in the paper the following day and found to my surprise that no mention of the death was made. Later that day the mystery was solved. The announcement was actually made on the news the day after my wife described it, and the person had only died the morning after she mentioned it.

In cases of this kind we see something which occurs precisely as we see it. There are also cases where what we see turns out to be a premonition of a future event. At the time there appears to be no difference. We see in vivid detail an aeroplane crashing, or a ship sinking. Then when we are about to board the plane or ship we cancel our voyage. This is what happened on the 'Titanic'. Sure enough the ship does sink, but here the 'view of the future' has served as a warning.

Now there appears to be a contradiction here. If the future exists in the present then we would not be able to change it. We would simply be reading the Akashic Records, the future which is recorded just like the past, and we would be bound by it. But it is clear from the premonition type of case that we can change the future, or alternatively that we are seeing something different at these times.

The point here is that if time is a unity and it co-exists in an eternal present, how can we change what is already present? If we have the free will to change it, how can it be already present? If we cannot change it, we do not have free will.

At this point it is necessary to distinguish between two things. Free will implies choice. It means that if we are presented with a situation, we have the power to follow one of a number of alternative paths. Now the mere fact that we can see the future, does not of itself prevent us from exercising this choice. If I see myself jumping over a cliff, that in itself does not mean I have no free will. I can have a preview of myself exercising my free will to jump off the cliff. It no more curtails my free will than showing a film of what people have done in the past. We can see them acting and we know what they are going to do. But at the time they were perfectly capable of making free choices.

But if the future has already happened, if it exists in the present, then what choice do we have? I read in the Akashic Records that on 21 November I will break my leg. I do not want to break my leg on that day, but in the unity of time, my leg is already broken. Then my free will is lost.

It is useless to start with the assumption that we must have free will. Free will is not inevitable. There is no logical reason why everything should not be determined. Perhaps the point is to accept our fate according to the laws of the universe and God's will instead of trying to fight against it.

The answer to this paradox, which is at the heart of the whole problem of free will and the ability to predict the future, lies in understanding the different levels of time. The confusion exists because only two levels, the so-called spiritual and physical, are considered, instead of the four levels that we have described in chapter 3. Inasmuch as space and time co-exist, time too exists on all four levels. In fact, we can simplify the situation here by regarding the higher mental and the astral as one.

True unity of time, where past, present and future co-exist, occurs only at the spiritual level. Here time is like a Chinese jar and here, if we could enter this realm, we could see absolute time. Here, where there is unity and perfection, there is no freedom. Here there simply is. This is the difference between men and angels. Angels, as the agents of God, inhabit the spiritual sphere. Angels, like God, have no freedom and have no need of it.

But when we look into the future we do not look directly at this spiritual level. We can only see as far as the intervening sphere, the astral or higher mental. This is the answer to our dilemma. We can only see the spiritual world in so far as it is reflected in the astral. We cannot see God face to face. And in so far as we do not see the spiritual sphere reflected in the astral, we see the reflection of our own minds.

When we practise divination, when we read the Akashic Records, when we travel in time, when we have dreams or premonitions, we are in the astral world. Sometimes we do see the future as it really is, sometimes we see but a reflection of what is in our own minds at the time. How close we are to the spiritual sphere depends on the purity of our own spirits.

This is why little children are usually the most intuitive, the most directly in touch with the spiritual state, the closest to God. 'I thank thee, O Father, Lord of heaven and earth, because thou hast hid these things from the wise and prudent, and hast revealed them unto babes.'[2] Divination is, therefore, getting in touch with the divine.

What so often happens with 'psychics' who purport to tell the future is that while they are sensitive to other people's minds, they do not usually pick up the spiritual level. Being more sensitive than pure they pick up what is in the other person's mind. This is reasonable enough provided we appreciate what is happening.

The purpose of using a system like the tarot or astrology is not to find out what will happen, but to get through to the other person's unconscious through the use of symbols and thus put them in touch with their own unconscious needs so that they can be helped to discover what they really want.

It is thus the client's unconscious aims and desires that the 'psychic' sees. Hence it is not necessarily the future as it actually turns out to be, but rather what is contained in the client's unconscious mind. Often the two coincide and one's unconscious aspirations do come to pass, but frequently they do not.

The art of divination is to get through to this astral or unconscious level and it is this, and this alone, that we can see. But the aim of the diviner is to get as near to the spiritual level as he can. It is this purity of motive, this personal 'divinity' which differentiates the true diviner from the fortune-teller who is little more than a psychic sponge.

The more closely in touch with his own spiritual source is the diviner, the more will what he sees in the astral or unconscious reflect the spiritual level rather than his own or his client's mind. As Israel Regardie has said:

> Divination (is) the art of obtaining at a moment's notice any required type of information regarding the outcome of certain actions or events. Fortune-telling so called is an abuse. The sole purpose of the art is to develop the intuitive faculties of the student to such an extent that eventually all technical methods of divination may be discarded. When that stage of development has been reached, mere reflection upon any problem will automatically evoke from the intuitive mechanism within the information required, with a degree of certainty and assurance that could never be acquired save from an inner psychic source.[3]

All the levels exist within us just as the quantum level co-exists with the material. In quantum physics, the waves that make up existence are indeterminate. They become determinate, they become particles, only when we observe them. In the astral, the waves are indeterminate. They reflect the spiritual. They become determinate, they enable us to tell the future, when we look at them.

Thus free will and fate co-exist. Freedom exists until we intervene. By asking the question we determine the answer. While we are on this Earth we cannot see the spirit, we cannot reach this level by ourselves. We can see only the reflection.

That we cannot see the spirit directly and that not even Jesus could while on Earth, he himself made clear. 'Heaven and Earth shall pass away: but my words shall not pass away. But of that day and that hour knoweth no man, no, not the angels which are in heaven, neither the Son, but the Father.'[4] And after his death he said: 'It is not for you to know the times or the seasons, which the Father hath put in his own power.'[5]

The conclusion is that although the future exists now, and has done since the beginning of time, on one level, the spiritual level, yet we on the physical level are not bound by it. We have freedom and we have will as human beings. But that is far from being the end of our quandary. Freedom we have in the sense of being able to choose. But the question that now arises is: should we exercise this choice? And to answer this question we need to examine the very concept of freedom. What is freedom? And, do we want freedom?

3 DAEMONIC, CHTHONIC POWERS – THE MEANING OF FREEDOM

> Here the impossible union
> Of spheres of existence is actual.
> Here the past and future
> Are conquered, and reconciled,
> Where action were otherwise movement
> Of that which is only moved
> And has in it no source of movement –
> Driven by daemonic, chthonic
> Powers.
> T.S. ELIOT, 'The Dry Salvages'

What is the nature of the freedom we appear to have? Does freedom mean that we can do whatever we like? Clearly this is not the case. Look at the Birth Chart illustrated in Figure 1.1. The person born at 7.18 a.m. on 15 July 1944 is stuck with that Birth Chart for life. He cannot escape from it. He will always have his Sun in Cancer in the 12th House, his Saturn square Neptune. To put it bluntly, he is fated with that Chart.

It is no good saying that he can be whatever he wants to be. He cannot have his Sun in Sagittarius. No effort of will can move his Moon into Gemini. Not all the understanding and belief in the universe will take his Venus out of the 12th House. So what freedom does he have? Have we solved the mystery of time and demonstrated that freedom is a reality only to show that it eludes us when we try to grasp it? Is it no more than the creation of a tantalizing God who dangles it before our eyes only to snatch it away when we approach it?

There is little point in asserting that we have freedom unless we know of what this freedom consists. On the face of it, the paradox remains. It is clear that we are not free, or not completely free. Indeed we are literally circumscribed by the wheel of life that is symbolized in the circle of our Horoscopes. We have a physical body, we have certain mental attitudes. Some of us are born crippled, blind or mentally retarded. We cannot fly, we cannot become champion athletes with only one leg.

Let me quote at this point a story which Franz Kafka tells in his novel *The Trial*, which I think serves as an appropriate parable:

> Before the Law stands a door-keeper. A man from the country comes up to this door-keeper and begs for admission to the Law. But the door-keeper tells him that he cannot grant him admission now. The man ponders this and then asks if he will be allowed to enter later. 'Possibly,' the door-keeper says, 'but not now.' Since the door leading to the Law is standing open as always and the door-keeper stands aside, the man bends down to look inside through the door. Seeing this, the door-keeper laughs and says: 'If it attracts you so much, go on and try to get in without my permission. But you must realise that I am powerful. And I'm only the lowest door-keeper. At every hall there is another door-keeper, each one more powerful than the last. Even I cannot bear to look at the third one.' The man from the country had not expected difficulties like this, for, he thinks, the Law is surely supposed to be accessible to everyone always, but when he looks more closely at the door-keeper in his fur coat, with his great sharp nose and his long, thin black Tartar beard, he decides it is better to wait until he receives permission to enter. The door-keeper gives him a stool and allows him to sit down to one side of the door. There he sits, day after day, and year after year.... During all these long years, the man watches the door-keeper almost continuously. He forgets the other door-keepers, the first one seems to be the only obstacle between him and admission to the Law.... In the end his eyes grow dim and he cannot tell whether it is really getting darker around him or whether it is just his

eyes deceiving him. But now he glimpses in the dark a radiance glowing inextinquishably from the door of the Law. He is not going to live much longer now. Before he dies all his experiences during the whole period of waiting merge in his head into one single question, which he has not yet asked the door-keeper. As he can no longer raise his stiffening body, he beckons the man over. The door-keeper has to bend down low to him, for the difference in size between them has changed very much to the man's disadvantage.

'What is it you want to know then?' asks the door-keeper. 'You're insatiable.' 'All men are intent on the Law,' says the man, 'but why is it that in all these many years no one other than myself has asked to enter?' The door-keeper realises that the man is nearing his end and that his hearing is fading, and in order to make himself heard he bellows at him: 'No one else could gain admission here, because this door was intended only for you. I shall now go and close it.'[6]

Each of us has his own path. And some have said that freedom means no more than accepting one's preordained fate willingly. This was the view of Jung: 'Freedom of will is the ability to do gladly that which I must do.' Carl Rogers, another psychologist, echoes this view: 'It is a freedom in which the individual chooses to fulfil himself by playing a responsible and voluntary part in bringing about the destined events of his world.'[7]

According to this opinion, one's life is prepared in advance. One has the freedom either to accept or reject it. In his *Meditations*, Marcus Aurelius wrote: 'Whatever may happen to thee, it was prepared to thee from all eternity; and the implication of cause was from eternity spinning the thread of thy being.'

We each have our own 'life myth'. This can be seen in the Horoscope. Indeed this is the Horoscope. There is no choice about this. Is the choice, then, simply in whether we accept that myth and live it knowingly or reject it and seek to follow another pattern? Jesus accepted his 'life myth' – to be crucified and to be the Saviour of Mankind. 'Take away this cup from me. Nevertheless, not my will, but thine, be done.'

He was tempted by Satan in the desert to become a temporal ruler. He could have chosen to fulfil the expectations that most of his countrymen, including his own disciples, had eagerly awaited in the Messiah. He could have raised up an army to drive the Romans from the Holy Land. Instead he accepted his fate. The choice was his and his alone.

As Whitmont expressed it: 'We may say that our complexes are the cards that fate has dealt us; with these cards and with no others we either win or lose the game, and if we behave as though we did not have them or if we ask for different ones we are beaten before we start.'[8] The Stoics sought to overcome the dilemma of fate and free will, the split between Heaven and Earth, in believing that the evil person was he who resisted the rule of nature, and that freedom lay in the harmony of nature and reason.

Let us turn the question around and ask why we have our Horoscopes to begin with. We assume that we are given our individual path in life. But perhaps we choose this path for ourselves. Perhaps our Horoscopes are the expression of our free choice. According to Kabbalist tradition, the soul is given freedom of choice and the plan of the task it is to perform in the world.

> The soul is then shown the model plan of its life to be lived, the people it will meet and the places it will pass through, knowing that its destiny is to realise the presence of God in that particular time and place within the physical Universe.

This certainly accords with the original meaning of the Horoscope as the 'right time' to be born. As Plotinus said: 'Every Soul has its hour (hora); when that strikes, the Soul descends and enters the body suitable to it.' We are therefore given our psychological and physical make-up, which can be seen in the Horoscope, because that is what we need in this incarnation. Thus there is a purpose in having 'the cards that fate has dealt us.'

What then are the eminent psychologists that I have quoted saying at the end of the day? That we have our characteristics willy-nilly so we might as well accept them? That we have the choice of liking them or lumping them? Seneca wrote: 'Fata volentem ducunt, trahunt nolentem.' And Jung paraphrased that statement when he remarked that human freedom rests upon the choice to walk upright on the appointed path, i.e. when we consent to walk on it, or to be dragged 'like cattle to the slaughterhouse' when we try to refuse.

However, this is not quite what is being said. Certainly there is no total freedom. Just as in the physical world there is no total freedom. In many ways we are limited. There are physical laws, and there are spiritual laws, and neither can be broken with impunity. We have the freedom to put our hand into the fire, and we have the power to place our souls into the spiritual fire.

When we get burned, we simply invoke the natural reaction that is inherent in these laws, according to the principle of Nemesis. It is not a question of being punished, or even so much of breaking a law. If we behave in a certain way, we will produce a certain reaction. The general spiritual laws are contained in the Kabbalah; the individual laws in Astrology, in the Horoscope.

The reason why we have freedom is because we are conscious. Consciousness enables us to make choices. The angels are not free. They have no need of freedom. Man is free because he is imperfect. And this is as it should be, for in his imperfection, he can achieve completeness.

Whitmont has expressed the position: 'Without consciousness of one's own potentials, limitations and necessities, freedom is a fancy concept.'[9] And Anthony Storr has written: 'We attain our greatest freedom when we recognise our limitations.'[10] But we can only exercise this freedom of choice when we truly utilize our conscious powers.

Until we are consciously aware of ourselves, our psychological make-up, then we have no power to exercise any choice. Self-understanding is therefore the first step to freedom. There can be no question of deciding whether to accept our 'life myth' unless we are first consciously aware of this 'life myth'. That is why we need to know ourselves – so that we can truly be ourselves. That is why the Horoscope is of such value – for it is a picture of ourselves.

Whatever we do, depends upon what we are. Many people,

perhaps most people, make the mistake of trying to run their lives the wrong way round. Instead of first trying to discover their individual role in life, they begin by trying to decide what they would like to do, and then attempt to adjust their lives so that they can put their intentions into practice.

In the few cases where a person is in touch with his inner self, he will be guided by his unconscious into his true direction. Otherwise he will be following a fruitless path – for it will not be his own. The right way is to find our own path first, by knowing ourselves, by being consciously in touch with our unconscious, and then to live up to that path.

If we are not conscious, then things happen to us in the outside world and we fail to recognize that these outside events are really mirroring our unconscious. As Jung has said:

> The psychological rule says that when an inner situation is not made conscious, it happens outside as fate. That is to say, when the individual remains undivided and does not become conscious of his inner contradictions, the world must perforce act out the conflict and be torn into opposite halves.[11]

In reality there is no difference between inner and outer. The unconscious contains our needs. We ought to be consciously aware of these needs otherwise the unconscious has a way of forcing them upon us. It is this union that allows us the freedom to choose. Emerson stated the principle thus:

> The secret of the world is the tie between person and event. The soul contains the event that shall befall it. The event is the print of your form. Events grow on the same stem with persons. Each creature puts forth from itself its own condition and sphere, as the slug sweats out its slimy house on the pear leaf. A man will see his character emitted in the events that seem to meet, but which exude from and accompany him.

At this stage, then, we have introduced the concept of consciousness. We consciously realize our 'life myth'. Does freedom now simply consist of being conscious of what should happen to us and then accepting it? At first glance it may appear to be little more than being awake during an operation.

But there is a profound paradox here which is clear from the apparently contradictory statements of Carl Rogers. On the one hand, he says:

> His (the close person's) behaviour is determined, but he is not free to make an effective choice. The fully functioning person, on the other hand, not only experiences, but utilizes, the most absolute freedom when he spontaneously, freely and voluntarily chooses and wills that which is absolutely determined.

On the other hand, he says: 'What I do in the next moment, and what I will do, grow out of that moment, and cannot be predicted in advance either by me or by others.' How can these two statements be reconciled?

If we accept ourselves as we are, then that is all that we can ever be. We cannot be anyone else, however much we might like to be. But once we really accept ourselves, then we do not have to do anything. By being, we inevitably become. We are in Tao, we are whole people, and our actions are a spontaneous development and a part of our being. We are a process.

This is the essential difference. It is one of attitude. And this is why what we will do cannot be foretold. It is an integral part of us. Our present and our future merge into one.

4 EACH IN HIS PRISON – THE WILL TO BE FREE

> I have heard the key
> Turn in the door and turn once only
> We think of the key, each in his prison
> Thinking of the key, each confirms a prison
> Only at nightfall, aethereal rumours
> Revive for a moment a broken Coriolanus.
>   T.S. Eliot, 'The Waste Land'

If freedom does exist, why are we in chains? At this stage another question must be faced: Do we want to be free?

We readily assume that freedom is desirable. It means doing whatever we like. We fail to appreciate the implications of responsibility and loneliness that are its inevitable corollary.

The simple truth is that most people are not free because they do not really want freedom.

Free will consists of two short words. We welcome the prospect of freedom. But we tend to forget about the will. Schopenhauer made the point when he said: 'We may have free will – but not the will to use it.' Freedom lies as much in our attitude as in our circumstances.

One person may regard his life as a prison while another will see the same circumstances as a fulfilment. As Richard Lovelace so poignantly wrote:

> Stone walls do not a prison make
> Nor iron bars a cage;
> Minds innocent and quiet take
> That for an hermitage.

The same appalling conditions of poverty and disease that have provided misery and despair to the vast majority of the inhabitants of Calcutta were welcomed by Mother Teresa. Many people who are paralysed, blind or physically handicapped are far freer in their spirits than those who have all the material advantages of life piled on them.

Often it is those who have everything who are the most greedy and discontented. Often it is those with the least advantages who succeed the best. Of course, one must first be aware of one's individual, unique path. The first step, therefore, is to find the purpose of one's life in this incarnation. And then to have the will to carry that purpose through.

The path to self-knowledge is the quest of myth. The path itself leads nowhere. We end where we started – with ourselves. But along the journey, in the journey itself, we come to recognize ourselves. We are what we are, but we can only get to know that which we are in our actions.

Freedom is a two-way process. First we have to break away from the womb, from authority, in order to achieve freedom towards individuality. This process is illustrated by the myth of the expulsion of Adam and Eve from Paradise, and the astrological parallels are of particular interest in the symbolism of this story.

In the beginning Adam and Eve lived in the walled garden of Paradise symbolizing the womb. At that time there was no differentiation and therefore no freedom. Then they were tempted by their minds, symbolized by the serpent, to go their own ways, in order to challenge the established authority of the Lord – the father-figure.

To be free they had to break away. It is of interest here that the Saturn figure represents both the authority from which they needed to separate, and also Satan the tempter who gave them the knowledge that enabled them to be free.

The paradox which is illustrated in the dual nature of Saturn is shown by the fact that it also represents our shadow. Thus the aim is not so much to get away from authority but to transform it from an outside source into a part of our inner structure. When we are really free, then we are our own authority, then of our own volition we can take up our personal Cross and follow the Lord again.

This is what Jung meant when he wrote: 'Unless one accepts one's fate . . . there is no individuation; one remains a mere accident, a mortal nothing.' After the initial separation, we can freely accept the lessons of life. And this too is what Jesus meant in saying: 'Take my yoke upon you, and learn of me; for I am meek and lowly in heart; and ye shall find rest unto your souls. For my yoke is easy, and my burden is light.'[12]

Because they disobeyed the commandments of God, Adam and Eve were expelled from Paradise. The umbilical cord was severed. Some people cannot achieve even this first necessary step towards freedom, that of Uranus. Such persons remain, literally or figuratively, tied to their womb-origins. Some never leave home, others marry parental-images, yet others remain like grown-up schoolboys coming back for the old reunions, desperately needing some authority, someone to tell them what to do, to take away the responsibility of running their lives.

Adam and Eve found themselves outside the gates of Paradise. The cherubims prevented their return to the garden containing the Tree of Life with their fiery swords. There was only one way they could go. Many get stuck at this point. They become rebels. They react negatively against all authority – their fathers, the government, the police, even structure in music and painting, without creating anything constructive to replace it.

These destroy, not to build up, but because they cannot reconcile Saturn within themselves. This is the stage of alienation – the lonely road through the desert. The point of opposing the father is not to be rid of the Saturn principle. The purpose of opposition is to see more clearly – to put in perspective, as in a mirror. Saturn as the shadow needs to be accepted and loved. Initially it needs to be broken down but only so that it can be built up again and transformed into a vital part of oneself. Christ leads us back to the Father through the Cross.

Those who are stuck at the negative Uranus juncture are not free. They have only 'a heap of broken images'. The next stage is to sacrifice ourselves to the love of God through Neptune. To learn to care, and not to care. To accept, and not to cling. To be prepared to give up our inner selves freely, without counting the cost. To give up everything, our lives, our concepts, our ideals.

The negative side of Neptune is the temptation to be rid of the burden of freedom in a masochistic way by becoming a martyr-figure. This effectively pushes the responsibility onto others – whether it be a person, a Guru, or an organization. What we need to do here is to accept our gifts and limitations as the necessary attributes of our characters.

This leads to the final stage, that of Pluto, where we try not to be anyone else, but to be truly ourselves. It is here that we need to use our wills ruthlessly, with all the power and determination of the pitiless but totally just god of the underworld.

Here we must tear away our dreams and face ourselves. Here we realize that what we dislike most is our own shadow. If we have the courage to do this, to accept ourselves as we really are, 'warts and all', and love ourselves as we are, then we shall be truly free. Then we can return to the Garden of Eden and taste of the Tree of Life.

We are back at the beginning. But the difference is that we have returned in the full light of consciousness. We are back where we started – but on a different level. First the mountain was one. To see the mountain, separation was necessary. Then union could be effected consciously. Once individuality for both halves had been achieved, then and only then could a marriage of the two take place.

The road to freedom is not an easy one. It requires a great

deal of courage to face oneself and to be oneself. First there is alienation when we are thrown out of Paradise. We oppose those in authority and learn to think for ourselves. We miss the warmth and security of home. It is much easier to accept other people's values and follow their expectations. It is much easier to blame others or outside circumstances than to accept that our problems originate within ourselves.

That is why the majority of people are not free. They like the sound of freedom. They demand their rights. But when it comes to accepting the responsibility that goes with it, when it comes to facing themselves as they really are, when it comes to treading their own lonely path and waiting outside their own gate, it is a very different matter. Then they turn sadly away.

But for those who turn away, life is no easier. Responsibility can be avoided up to a point. But whether they like it or not, they are still themselves and they cannot get away from themselves. If we refuse to accept what is inside the wheel of our Horoscope, then we simply turn with the wheel oblivious to reality. Nothing is changed. We may close our eyes, but the wheel still turns.

The same circumstances will happen in any case. What matters is not what occurs but how we experience what occurs. That is the difference between freedom and fate. Pluto will square Mercury in Figure 1.1 on 6 February 1986. That can be seen from the day of birth. There is no avoiding it. It is that person's fate. But what meaning, if any, will the owner of that Horoscope give to that contact? How will he experience it — freely and consciously, or with his eyes closed?

The planetary contacts are made to the Horoscope throughout our lives because we need to encounter certain experiences. Experiences are necessary. If we try to avoid them, we miss the point. We need to evolve in order to grow, to become more as we really are, and sometimes this process is a painful one.

By seeking to avoid the process, we are not cheating fate. We cheat only ourselves. We literally spend our lives running away from our own shadow. Freedom exists in the ability to give crises either a meaning of growth and fulfilment or a meaning of frustration and helplessness. What matters is the meaning of what happens — why does it happen? Why is Pluto going to square Mercury in 1986?

As Whitmont has written:

> The Self's aid rather than its obstruction may be summoned by an attitude which asks: What does this situation ask of me or intend to teach me? How may I serve this problem for the sake of life and the transpersonal value? Rather than: What can I get out of this in terms of personal gain.[13]

Or as Frankl has put it:

> As each situation in life represents a challenge to man and presents a problem for him to solve, the question of the meaning of life may actually be reversed. Ultimately man should not ask what the meaning of life is, but rather must recognise that it is HE who is asked. In a word, each man is questioned by life: to life he can only respond by being responsible... responsibleness is the very essence of human existence. So one should not search for an abstract meaning of life. Everyone has his own specific vocation or mission in life; everyone must carry out a concrete assignment that demands fulfillment. Therein he cannot be replaced, nor can his life be repeated. Thus everyone's task is as unique as is his specific opportunity to implement it.

We each have our own individual path. That path is symbolized by the Horoscope. That is us. If we develop naturally, according to our inherent pattern, then we shall be ourselves. We do not have to look up every future transit and work out which of several possibilities we should take. We need to be whole, in Tao, where conscious and unconscious are one. Then we will inevitably do what is right in any particular set of circumstances, simply because doing is part of being.

The free will we have is a matter of whether or not we align our wills with the divine pattern that is our real selves, or our spiritual or archetypal nature. It is not a question of being passive. On the contrary, it requires a good deal of will power to be constantly in touch with our real selves.

The aim then is first to find our true pattern which is symbolized by the Horoscope. And secondly to align ourselves with this pattern so that our will and God's will are united. In other words our physical level is united with our spiritual level or our Divine Spark. Then if we are one with the universe, on what can we exercise our free will? If we are free, we just are. Then we cannot not be free.

5 THE FRUIT OF THE VINE – FATE AND FREE WILL IN ASTROLOGY

> And God said
> Prophesy to the wind, to the wind only for only
> The wind will listen.
> T.S. Eliot, 'Ash-Wednesday, 1930'

We should now be in a position to answer the question: Can Astrology predict the future? As we have seen, this question is not as straightforward as it originally appeared. First, there is the general question as to whether it is possible to foretell the future. Second, there is the specific question as to whether astrologers can foretell the future, assuming the first question is answered in the affirmative.

We have resolved the paradox implicit in the first question by distinguishing between the different worlds or levels that exist. Only on the spiritual, or archetypal, level is there true unity of time and space. Here the past, present and future combine in one timeless moment. If we could attain this state then we could see the future as assuredly as we can the present.

We can achieve this state of 'suchness' and see the future on rare, mystic occasions. Then, although we cannot say how, we just know. Jung was once asked if he believed in God. 'No,' he began slowly, 'I do not believe in God.' There was a moment of stunned silence, before he continued: 'I know.'

This is the experience of the Absolute, the Union with God. 'I know that my redeemer liveth.' It is a vision of totality when existence becomes one and we have no doubt. Anyone who has had an experience like this simply knows, even though he cannot explain or share his experience.

On the physical level we are free even though we rarely exercise that freedom. We are free to choose our path, free in our attitude towards our lives. The end result may be the same whichever path we take, but in spiritual terms the difference is immense.

Jesus had the freedom to abrogate his destiny and shun the Cross. Instead of becoming the Saviour of mankind, he might have become a temporal ruler of a free Israel. Then the Romans may have marched on his new kingdom and crucified him for his political activities. On the material level he would have ended up on the cross in any event. But if he had chosen the latter path, would that Cross now be a sacred symbol the world over?

We cannot tell which path a person will choose in physical terms. On this level we have the freedom to decide our future. So, strictly speaking, the second question does not arise. Nevertheless, even though the future cannot be told in an absolute sense, some kind of future can be predicted on the material level, and it is important to see what does happen in this area of the astrologer's art.

For there is no doubt that the astrologer, like the astronomer, can tell without any doubt precisely where the planets will be in the sky at any particular moment in the future. In this sense he can predict, and predict accurately. There is not the slightest doubt that on 26 January 1989, Uranus will occupy the area of the ecliptic known as 3 degrees 12 minutes of Capricorn which is directly opposite Saturn's place in the Horoscope illustrated in Figure 1.1. Any astrologer can tell us this, and that mundane prediction, unless the solar system is disrupted in the meantime, is incontestable.

But the trouble arises when astrologers attempt to interpret the material phenomena. And it is at this point that it is vital to appreciate the meaning and purpose of Astrology if the art is to be used correctly. It is useless to say that the future cannot be predicted at all or that the astrologer should leave prediction alone as some astrologers have done.

This is simply an attempt to run away from the problem. We know perfectly well that in January 1989 Uranus will oppose Mr X's natal Saturn, and that in January 1896 Uranus would have been 90 degrees from Saturn in the Horoscope illustrated in Figure 2.1. What the client wants to know in both of these cases is the significance of the planetary contacts at these times. What will these contacts mean to Mr X and to Mr Y?

Thus the question that the astrologer should be trying to

answer is what is the meaning of a particular planetary contact to an individual client. What most astrologers do in practice however, is something quite different. Instead of looking for meaning in terms of the individual they look for some general proposition which may or may not have any relevance to the actual client they are considering.

This is because these astrologers have based their methods on what they believe to be 'scientific' methodology. These methods may be appropriate for scientists but that does not automatically make them relevant for astrologers. What happens is that astrologers look for some general principle based on past statistical evidence. They look at thousands of Uranian contacts that have occurred in the past and find that the most common occurrence is some kind of 'change'. Therefore there is likely to be a change in the person's life.

Then by breaking down the varieties of change they can state the probability of any particular kind of change occurring. Now statistics do have a role to play in certain areas of knowledge, but used in the wrong circumstances they can be totally inappropriate and misleading.

In Astrology we are talking about individuals, not groups. The whole meaning and purpose of Astrology is lost if one tries to tell the future of an individual on the basis of statistics. And not only is the point lost but a great deal of harm can be done. Harm to the individual client who is not treated as an individual but as a cog in a machine, and harm to the astrologer who fails to use his art correctly.

The question is what does Uranus opposing her natal Venus mean to Mrs Jones? As I have stressed throughout this book, Astrology is a combination of conscious and unconscious. We need to use the conscious to get through to the unconscious. The symbols used in Astrology should be used intuitively. This is why methods like the Tarot and the I Ching are better for prediction than Astrology. Being more elastic, they enable us to get through to the unconscious more easily.

By using our conscious powers too readily we can actually block off our predictive ability. We end up by closing the link between conscious and unconscious. Thus we fail to see the inherent meaning in the symbols. The future should grow out of the present and the past as part of a total organism.

Although we tend to see the Birth Chart as separate from the future directions, in reality the latter are contained in the former. The Birth Chart should be regarded as a state of being, representing what we need in this incarnation. It is not static, nor is it cut off or isolated from the future. The moment of time symbolized in the Birth Chart flows into the next moment.

We can see the Birth Chart as the Self, as space. And we can see directions[14] as destiny or fulfilment, as time. Both are but two ways of looking at the same thing – the space/time continuum. Destiny is thus the opportunity to fulfil one's Self – one's Birth Chart.

Directions give us freedom by demanding choice and action, by giving us the opportunity to become what we really are. In order to develop we need to change – even though the purpose of change is to become more as we are but on another level. We need to realize the selves we are from the beginning. Strictly speaking we do not need to wait for certain directions in order to evolve and become our true selves.

But there is a time for everything. There are certain natural times when it is easier and more appropriate to understand certain of our potentials and needs, and it is at these particular times that we can most naturally develop the qualities inherent in the Birth Chart. So it is a question of foretelling the quality of the times in the future – so that the individual can get in touch with those times.

What we should be asking when we look at directions is: What experience does *this individual* need? When should he experience what he needs? We need to make adjustments to bring about balance. If we refuse to acknowledge the need for change, the lessons become more drastic. If we have already learned them they will have little effect. We can see when these adjustments need to be made by looking at the directions. But the need to make the adjustments is contained in the Birth Chart from the very moment of birth.

Many people look at Uranus transiting a natal Venus as something happening to Mrs Jones when she is forty-five years old. Things may appear to 'happen' to people, but as Jung pointed out that is the result of the individual being undivided. Then, when there is no differentiation between conscious and unconscious, instead of understanding the meaning of the time, the inner is projected onto the outside world to make things 'happen'.

So Mrs Jones may get divorced when Uranus opposes her Venus. But that is not the point. That occurrence may take place if she is unaware. It may equally be the result of a conscious decision. The point is to make her aware by helping her to understand what she needs at that particular time, based upon her individual character as symbolized by her Horoscope.

Even then she may need to be divorced, just as Jesus needed to be crucified. On the other hand she may not. The actual happening, if there is one, should be the materialization of an inner experience. Sometimes, the experience comes from the occurrence. And although this is really the wrong way round at least one can learn in this way.

The purpose of predictive Astrology is to put people in touch with the times in the future so that they can be helped to use these times. To make them a part of those times. To say that prediction is no part of Astrology is as inconsistent as saying that time is irrelevant to Astrology.

To get in touch with the inner meaning of the times, one needs to use the unconscious, for the planetary contacts affect the individual's unconscious. Therefore the astrologer needs to get through to the client's unconscious with his own unconscious or intuitive powers. It is only once this stage is reached that the client, and the astrologer, can consciously understand the situation. The more one ties down predictive techniques, the more rigid they are, the less scope there is for the intuition to work. This is a grave practical problem today among some astrologers who are afraid to use their intuition and end up trying to imitate scientists in one branch of Astrology where scientific methodology is inappropriate.

Great care needs to be taken in using Astrology and this applies particularly to prediction. We should not be afraid of the future any more than of the present. If we are in touch with our selves, then we shall inevitably become what we are. The future and the present blend into one and then we need only ask the question for the answer to come.

Why do we need Astrology then? Because we are not in touch with our selves. If we were whole we would not need a doctor. If we were in a state of being, of Tao or grace, we would not need Astrology. Astrology, used correctly, can help people to be in this state, but astrologers first need to be aware of the goal.

The client, too must be aware. Will is as important as freedom as we have pointed out. The more exact one purports to be, however altruistic the motive, the less freedom there is for the client to exercise his own will. Many clients come to astrologers, not because they want to understand themselves, but because they want someone to take away their responsibility. Freedom is the one thing they do not want.

It is all too easy to play God with people like this for that is what they expect. It is very easy to make suggestions, however unintentional, which may have unfortunate results. At the end of the day, the quality of the astrologer's predictions will depend on the quality of his own spiritual state. The nearer the astrologer is to divine ground, the nearer will he be to the truth. He too, needs to be in a state of Tao and to approach his art and his fellow human beings with reverence, humility and love if he is to be of real help to them.

CHAPTER 6
The firmament – reality and perception

If the doors of perception were cleansed every thing would appear to man as it is, infinite.

WILLIAM BLAKE

Before we can begin to understand the meaning of a Horoscope, we must learn to see it in the right way. The aim is to see the essence behind the outer form, but the problem that arises is that what we see depends upon the way we perceive it.

I have already touched briefly on the role of the mind as the link between the essence of a thing, or the archetypal level, and the material manifestation of that thing. In this chapter I shall examine the mind as reality structurer in more detail.

We cannot exclude ourselves from reality. It is clear at the very least that there is an interaction between that which is perceived and those who perceive. If a dozen artists paint a landscape, each will produce a different composition depending on his way of using his senses. What then is the reality that each sees?

In music, the harmonious combinations of different notes result when their frequencies are in certain numerical ratios. The notes are harmonious to us because of our senses. It is we who create, or pick out, what is harmonious to us.

And we who perceive are affected by the way we have been taught to perceive. We all learn to perceive as children. But although the ability to perceive is innate, the way in which we perceive is something that is learned. We learn to see in three dimensions, we are taught to choose certain elements, and to ignore others.

As humans we rely mainly on our visual sense and therefore our sense of space is limited. A sensation which is based on sight is necessarily local and circumscribed within the bounds of a specific place. Sound, on the other hand, is not localized in this way and if we used our sense of hearing rather than that of sight we would not feel the need to localize the waves that we react to.

There is also a basic difference between cultures, in particular between east and west. In the Sumerian creation myth I quoted in chapter 1, it will be recalled that the mountain was cut in half. But the two halves still made up the whole of the mountain.

Now there is a vital distinction in the western version of the creation story. In Judeao-Christian mythology God also began His work by dividing Heaven and Earth. But in the western myth, God placed a firmament between the two halves.

This distinction is of the greatest significance between two quite different ways of seeing the world. In the Sumerian story there is division in unity, but in the biblical version there is also separation between Heaven and Earth. In the west, man's goal is unity, the integration of the personality, or individuation as Jung has called it. But the way to reach this goal is through divergence. Before there can be individuation, there must be individuality, and this can only be attained through separation.

The aim in the west is containment, not by eliminating or cancelling out duality, but by integrating it within the whole. While we are on the physical level, we are governed by the laws of duality. This is the way we see in accordance with our senses. Only when we reach the spiritual, or inner, level, are we united. But because there is only one reality, unity and duality are the same. This paradox lies at the very root of learning to see.

How then do we reach the essence of a thing? When we see a rose only on the physical level, we blend our physical senses with the physical senses of the rose. When we see the rose on an inner level, we blend our archetypal or spiritual centre with that of the rose. In this way we capture the essence of the subject.

This means learning to see in a new way. The astrologer as much as the artist must first unlearn his old habits. William Blake, that great spiritual painter, said of the eye: 'I look through it, not with it.' When we see physical matter according to our physical perception we are in a state of duality. When we learn to see the unity behind the physical aspect, we also see the essence. This inner vision is a part of all of us because we all have a spiritual as well as a physical nature, although in most of us it is undeveloped.

Someone asked Blake what he saw when he looked at the Sun. ' "What," it will be questioned, "when the sun rises, do you not see a round disk of fire somewhat like a guinea?" ' Blake replied: 'O no, no. I see an innumerable company of the heavenly host crying, "Holy, Holy, Holy is the Lord God Almighty!" ' There is nothing to prevent us from seeing the soul in the Horoscope or in any aspect of nature. It is our old, habitual patterns of perception that block the unity between inner and outer and shield the glory from our eyes.

1 THIS LIFE'S FIVE WINDOWS – DUALITY, THE WAY WE SEE

> This life's five windows of the soul
> Distorts the Heavens from pole to pole
> And lead you to believe a lie
> When you see with, not thro', the eye.
> WILLIAM BLAKE

The fact that we cannot exclude ourselves from the nature of reality, is now being appreciated by physicists. 'Access to the physical world,' says Zukav, 'is through experience. The common denominator of all experience is the 'I' that does the experiencing. In short, what we experience is not external reality, but our INTERACTION with it.'[1]

Naturally logical thinking and analysis is of the greatest importance in science, as indeed it is in Astrology. But it is necessary to have an idea of the whole as well as the parts. Unless the scientist knows what he is looking for, he will be unable to begin his experiments. And unless he can recognize the meaning in the mass of detail when he sees it, the truth will never be revealed.

The point is to use both functions, the rational and the intuitive, simultaneously. Although this is a simplified picture, our physical brains are divided into the left half which is concerned with linear, rational thinking and the right half which functions in an intuitive manner.

There has been much fruitless argument about which side is of greater importance. The scientist is blamed for missing the meaning of the universe, the mystic for being unable to explain his vision. Both are as important and as necessary as the other. Both are contained in us, and thus it is necessary to recognize that the way we perceive is in accordance with both of these functions.

If we combine the two, we can learn to see the whole as well as the parts and recognize that they are the same. As the Chuang-Tzu says:

> This point is the point of the law; it is the motionless centre of a circumference on the rim of which all contingencies, distinctions and individualities resolve; and from it only infinity is to be seen, which is neither this nor that, nor yes nor no. To see all in the yet undifferentiated primordial unity, or from such a distance that all melts into one, this is true intelligence.

The left side of the brain dissects. It asks the questions. It looks for cause and effect in a scientific manner. It insists on explanation. The right side looks for meaning, for wholeness in the images – paradox and ambiguity. As R.H. Blyth has said: 'The intellect can understand any part of a thing as a part, but not as a whole. It can understand anything which God is not.'

Part of this duality is to assume that the question and the answer are different. But in appreciating the unity of the division, we see that the question itself is the answer. It is the purpose of the Japanese koan, such as 'What is the sound of hand clapping?' to illustrate this paradox.

Most people see only with their eyes, and even then they see only what they want to see. When we see through our senses, then we are ready to take the final paradoxical step towards the spiritual level which is true union. 'When is a man in mere understanding?' asks Meister Eckhart. 'I answer, when he sees one thing separate from another. And when is a man above understanding? That I can tell you: when a man sees All in all, then a man stands beyond mere understanding.'

2 OBJECTIVE AND SUBJECTIVE UNIVERSE

> He thought he saw an Elephant,
> That practised on a fife:
> He looked again, and found it was
> A letter from his wife.
> 'At length I realise,' he said,
> The bitterness of life.
>
> Lewis Carroll

Having learned how to see, we should be in a better position to discover the reality of what we see. What is 'out there'? How does it differ, if at all, from what is 'in here'? Specifically in astrological terms, what is the nature of the events that appear to happen to us? Have the factors in the Horoscope an independent reality? Has the Moon in Taurus in Figure 1.1 and Figure 2.1 any meaning of its own?

The old assumption of an objective universe that was one of the cornerstones of scientific thought is now being eroded. But, as we have seen, the belief in something 'out there' which is separate from the minds that perceive it, is one that will not die easily however much scientists assert the contrary.

Our minds inevitably act as a filter through which reality as we know it is processed. Our own bodies are but a structured way of perceiving matter. In a sense we create our own reality with our minds. This can be illustrated not only by the common experience of dreams and the less frequent experience of astral travel, but also by what occurs when we die. It has been recorded that people frequently do not realize for some time that they are dead. They create a world similar to the one they have inhabited while they were alive – and are unable to tell the difference.

Thus it is not merely a question of the universe being affected by the way we see it. We ourselves play a positive role in creating what we see. Matter is real to us as human beings because it is structured in a certain way by our senses. We see the planets because we as humans tune into the frequency of visible light. Other forms of life, who tune into the audible part of the electromagnetic spectrum, would hear the planets instead.

There has been a tendency to swing in two opposite directions. To say either that the physical world does not exist because it is simply the way we sense it, or to say that it does exist but that our minds which perceive it are not real. The resolution of this question is of great importance in deciding whether the Signs of the Zodiac have an objective reality or whether they are purely symbolic.

The pattern we see is created and conditioned by our perceptions. We see the constellations although there is nothing connecting the stars in the same way that our minds form an image from a photograph which is really made up of thousands of separate dots.

It has been suggested that our minds alter the 'super-hologram of reality'[2] but this in itself implies that there is some objective reality to alter and the question remains as to the nature of this reality. Our consciousness contains a 'reality-structurer', a neurophysical mechanism which inevitably affects reality and it may therefore be said that our minds are part of a complex feedback process where inner and outer affect each other.

We can only perceive the universe in accordance with our senses. But, as we stressed in the last section of this chapter, there is a vital distinction in the way we use our senses. If we get stuck on the form then we shall only see the outer physical shell. Then we shall only see the planets, the Signs of the Zodiac, as physical objects, as things with a definite meaning.

But if we learn to see through our senses, like Blake, we shall be able to see the essence of the planets and the Signs. Then we can see behind the outer form.

This does not mean that the physical world is unreal. This is a conclusion that scientists have come to as a result of the assumption that a thing can only be one thing at a time. Being forced to accept that the mind is real, and that the world is as it is because that is the way we subjectively see it, they then say that the whole physical world is an illusion.

However there is no need to accept this either/or presupposition. Indeed this is one of the mistaken conclusions of the scientific mind. The physical world, the world we perceive, is real for us because that is the way we do perceive it. A brick is real enough when it lands on our head but it is the experience of the brick which matters to the astrologer. It is this that he needs to grasp behind the material manifestation.

If we learn to experience as well as see we shall be less bound by our physical senses. Seeing and experiencing are two distinct things. Most people who see the Sun rise do not experience it. Most astrologers who talk of a Moon-Venus conjunction have not even seen the phenomenon in the sky, yet alone experienced it as a physical and spiritual reality.

If we forget our preconceived ideas and just open our eyes, or close our eyes and open our minds, we shall have a chance of experiencing the truth. The great service of myth in personalizing and naming the forces that exist in the universe has been to make people aware of their reality. We do not have to call the force of anger Mars or Geburah, but these names and the visual symbols that accompany them enable us to experience the underlying power that is the reality behind the image.

3 A HEAP OF BROKEN IMAGES – SYMBOLS AND MODELS

> What are the roots that clutch, what branches grow
> Out of this stony rubbish? Son of man,
> You cannot say, or guess, for you know only
> A heap of broken images.
>
> T.S. ELIOT, 'The Waste Land'

The mind is the surface on which is reflected the reality known to us as experience. And the mind works by making models. As Edward Whitmont has written: 'Consciousness based upon conceptualised mental functioning is a relatively late, secondary form of mental development. The basic or original unit of mental functioning is the image. Concepts are fashioned out of images through the activity of abstraction which is a thought process.'[3]

If we go back to our model of the different planes of existence in chapter 3, we shall recall that the highest level is the archetypal. But we cannot see archetypes. We cannot see God. We cannot see fear or power or justice. Therefore we need to form a mental image of these archetypal forces so that we can see them. This does not of course mean that they do not exist. That is the basic fallacy of the materialist. Indeed it is more true to say that the archetype is the only reality. What we see and measure is the outer shell.

Thus what we perceive is but a mental image. Jung has said: 'Everything thought, felt or perceived is a psychic image, and the world exists only so far as we are able to produce an image of it.'

These models are the formation of the rational mind. Only when they become symbols are they formed by the power of the intuitive faculties. This can easily be forgotten, particularly in science where models are frequently used. But the atom in physics, the personality in psychology, the Horoscope in Astrology, are all models. As such they are useful. But neither the atom, the personality, nor the Horoscope, can be seen. They are not exact; they are approximations.

At the present time, models in science are indeterminate because man's views are indeterminate. At one time Astrology was determinate and fatalistic. Now it is based more upon intuition, psychology, spiritual truth.

Our minds do not originate. What the mind conceives or experiences exists in some dimension. The archetypes exist as essences. From these seeds, our minds create their images and clothe their nakedness. The archetypes then are analogous to brass rubbings. We make them, with our minds, gradually appear. They pre-exist, but we cannot see them.

Because the emphasis in the east is on the intuitive faculties, they see more directly than we in the west. But they, too, need images even though they are more direct than ours. They do not need the ritual and the symbolic drama that has been built up in the west and that appeals to our senses and material viewpoint. We, on the other hand, need to clothe our archetypes with richly embroidered apparel, with many layers of meaning. That is why Astrology, combined with the Kabbalah and the Tarot, is especially appropriate for our culture.

4 SHAPE WITHOUT FORM – WHAT WE SEE IN THE HOROSCOPE

> Shape without form, shade without colour,
> Paralysed force, gesture without motion.
> T.S. Eliot, 'The Hollow Men'

If we accept that reality is as we perceive it, then the importance of seeing in the right way will be apparent. It is useless for astrologers to complain of scientific materialism if astrologers themselves do the same as the scientists. It is easy to criticise others for looking at the world as if it is 'out there' but this is just what we have been taught to do.

The accepted method of learning Astrology is the scientific method. We look at a Horoscope as if it is something apart from ourselves. We take it to pieces, analyse each factor. We ask the meaning of the Sun in Cancer, the Moon in Taurus square Jupiter, and Neptune in the 3rd House.

Then we dissect the pieces even further. We look at the midpoints, direct and indirect, between the Sun and Moon, at the Moon's nodes, the asteroids, the arabian parts. On no account must we fail to take account of the 7th and 9th harmonics, and so on ad infinitum.

It has been said, by psychologists as well as astrologers, that Astrology is the best form of psychological evaluation because it is objective. The factors in a Horoscope have a fixed and definite meaning and all one has to do is to read the meaning of these separate factors like a computer print-out. This is nonsense and like much nonsense it is founded on a partial truth. The partial truth is that the pictorial Horoscope is something that does not change.

The Horoscope is a graphic picture of the planets which are actually in the sky at the moment of birth. Astronomically the data do not change. The Horoscope illustrated in Figure 1.1 will be no different in itself no matter who is looking at it. But there is no fixed meaning in the various factors.

The Horoscope is a picture and, as in a painting, one colour can be extracted and analysed, say it is cadmium red mixed with a small part of yellow ochre and a touch of burnt sienna. But when that colour is looked at in the context of the painting as a whole it will be quite different from the identical colour in another painting because each separate factor is affected by and is a part of the whole.

Our knowledge of the separate factors in Astrology is gained by the use of statistics and averages. But, as we have seen, statistics tell us nothing about the individual and it is the individual that we are looking at. The fact that 568 men with their Sun in Cancer are fat and shy, while 392 are tenacious and moody may be of great interest to a statistician. But however valid these elements are in themselves, they are of no more practical use to a living person than an extract of his liver would be in isolation from the rest of his body. No two moments of time are the same. The pattern of the heavens will always be different. Each moment, like each person, is unique.

In a way the very fixity of the data in a Horoscope is misleading. Just because the picture is definite, it can lead to the assumption that the person described by that picture is immutable. For our minds can remain fixed on the symbols themselves instead of seeing through them.

It is not the Sun in Cancer in itself, as a rational image, that describes the person. It is the force behind this symbol. The Sun in Cancer is no more than a gate, a psychic image, leading us to the inner meaning. One does not expect to read a person like a book if one is talking to him, yet this is just what many astrologers expect to do with a Birth Chart.

The way to the symbolic truth contained in the Horoscope is through the intuition. No amount of rational thought will enable us to understand the real meaning of the symbols. This does not mean that we should not use our rational faculties. Indeed we should. But they should be used together with the intuitive powers. Both are halves of one whole – Heaven and Earth, the one mountain of Anki.

Certainly we need to look at the parts, we need to analyse, to see what Mercury conjunct Pluto in Leo in the 1st House means. But having analysed the parts, we must go on to see the whole. And seeing the whole is not a question of piecing the separate parts together like a jigsaw. This is the fallacy. It is seeing in a new way.

In order to use our intuitive powers, we need to let go, to sink into the void. There are two ways of achieving this. One is through meditation. Meditation in this sense means the concentrated examination of an image, and while the mind is fixed upon it, relaxing the conscious mind and allowing ideas to rise up around it from the unconscious.

The alternative way is to soak the mind with all the separate factors, thus using the rational faculties at the outset. Then the mind is switched off and the meaning comes when we cease to think consciously about the image. The question travels from the left to the right side of the brain and the answer comes intuitively.

Gradually it will be found that one can see the Horoscope as a whole without needing the mental aides that are contained within it. For to a large extent that is what the factors in the Horoscope are. They are like markers which set off the intuitive powers, like a crystal ball which is used to concentrate the mind and allow the intuition free play. Eventually we should get to the point where the Birth Chart is like a crystal ball.

If one looks at good astrologers at work this is just what does happen. The astrologer will look at the Chart and give an accurate assessment of the individual's character. Asked for reasons for his assessment, he will pick on certain factors and it will be apparent that these factors are no more than rationalizations for the intuitive approach.

What is needed is a dialogue by way of the symbolic forms which are put forth from the unconscious mind and recognized by the conscious. In this way the intuitive and the rational are brought together. And in learning to see in this way, we will have learned a great message from Astrology for we shall be more truly in touch with ourselves.

Then we shall see what the Horoscope really contains. It has been asked if we can see the Self or God in the Horoscope. If we saw in the right way we would not ask this question. If we use only our rational powers then we shall see what is called in the east, Samsara – the Wheel of Becoming. If we use our intuitive powers we shall see Nirvana or Suchness. The two are the same. Which we see depends on how we perceive.

We are our Selves. The Self or God is not in us – it *is* us. It is our total being, our complete selves. The trouble arises in the west because doing is separated from being, a person from his actions. We can ask the same question about transubstantiation. Does the bread and the wine change into the body and blood of Christ? Neither we nor the bread change. We and it are Christ. We become what we are. The archetypal symbol or mandala which is the Horoscope allows our inner self to link intuitively with the inner self of the Horoscope. The Horoscope is what we are and it is that which we become.

CHAPTER 7
Jacob's ladder

Lord, thou wilt be no man's till he has become thine own.
St Augustine

Between Heaven and Earth lies the human psyche and it is this which we shall now examine. What is the correlation in human terms between the planets 'out there' and the individual who is born at a certain time? Why does the pattern formed in the sky at the moment of birth describe the human psyche?

There is an intimate and integral connection between the universe and ourselves which lies at the very basis of Astrology. It is the nature of this connection in human terms that provides meaning to our lives. What meaning was there for the person born at 7.57 p.m. on 26 July 1875 whose Horoscope is illustrated in Figure 2.1, when Uranus passed over his Ascendant and Saturn opposed his Midheaven in 1913?

Confucius said that it is only when the earthly patterns match Heaven's that the spiritual beings which make up Heaven can be drawn into the drama of man and made to operate helpfully on earth.

At the moment of birth the pattern in the heavens and on earth are aligned. Inner and outer are united. The mountain is one. But the union is an unconscious one. Once the mountain is cut in half, the top and the bottom must be consciously reunited.

The mountain needs to be divided. Before we can be consciously aware of our needs, and hence before we can be free to control our lives, we need to separate the conscious from the unconscious. Jung makes the point in a passage I have already quoted when he says that when an inner situation is not made conscious, it happens outside as fate. 'That is to say, when the individual remains undivided and does not become conscious of his inner contradictions, the world must perforce act out the conflict.'

Whatever exists in a person's Horoscope is a part of him and a part of the pattern of the universe into which he is born. If Mars lies in the 7th House of his Horoscope then he needs to be consciously in touch with that factor. If he is not in touch with it, then it will rise up to meet him.

Whatever appears as a manifestation of that factor will ask him to find its meaning and confront him like the sphinx in the desert. It may appear on a mundane level in the form of a violent partner. That form, the physical shape that this symbol has taken, will enable him to express the energy symbolized therein, perhaps by making him aware of his need to be assertive in his relationships.

That particular individual may need a violent partner to make him consciously aware of an aspect of his nature, just as Jesus needed to be crucified in order to reconcile himself with his shadow. He may not. The outer form can provide the realization of the inner meaning or the inner meaning of the factor can be gained more directly. How closely the individual is in touch with the essence of his Horoscope depends on how closely aligned are the earthly and heavenly patterns for him.

1 THE UNION OF CONSCIOUS AND UNCONSCIOUS

What after all, did the king do? He watched his conduct carefully and turned his face southward solemnly. Nothing more.

CONFUCIUS

The need to understand the nature of man is a prerequisite for understanding the nature of reality, for the separation that exists in the world is a reflection of the separation that exists in ourselves. So long as we are divided, we shall continue to see the world as divided.

Only by understanding our own minds and uniting the two pillars of consciousness and unconsciousness can we achieve the union and integration of ourselves that will enable us to see the world as a united and integrated place.

The question for man is how he can integrate consciousness, his more recent acquisition, with unconsciousness, his oldest, and thus unite Heaven and Earth within himself. The original function was the unconscious. Mother Earth, Gaia, gave birth to Ouranos, Heaven, and then married her celestial son.

This does not imply that the unconscious function is superior, any more than is the conscious. A marriage should be between two equal partners, each accepting and respecting the other, and both functions are as necessary as each other.

The unconscious, as the original function, contains our deepest needs. It is the repository of our primal requirements. If we are in touch with this deep substratum of ourselves, then we instinctively feel connected with nature as a whole. So it is that animals, and to a lesser extent primitive peoples, are more in touch with nature.

It was for this reason that our ancestors felt the correspondence between themselves and the forces of nature before consciousness was developed. But it is not enough to be unconscious. Then we remain on the level of the animals and we are unable to control our lives.

In some ways that may appear to be no bad thing, for the control of our environment is rapidly leading to its destruction. Many have looked back with longing at the halcyon days of primitive living. But if we want freedom, we must accept consciousness. We must have the freedom to create our own Heaven or Hell on earth. Life for primitive man may have had its advantages, but he was ruled as much by the fear of nature as by its love.

For better or for worse, Adam and Eve needed to eat of the Tree of Knowledge. They could not remain forever in the safety of the walled garden. They had to accept consciousness and make their own way into the world in order to see objectively.

The danger of separation lies in losing touch with the unconscious. We grow so far from our origins that, like Ulysses on his voyage, we quite forget our homes. We lose touch with our roots. Like astronauts whose ties with their spacecraft have been severed, we find ourselves unable to return to Mother Earth.

This is what has happened as the conscious powers have been developed. In western civilization in particular, the emphasis has been more and more on the yang side of life; on the rational, objective, mental functions, as opposed to the yin side, the intuitive powers of understanding and immediate experience. On the positive, masculine, extrovert values as opposed to the negative, feminine, introvert needs. On science instead of art and spiritual truth.

I should make it clear that in emphasizing the role of the unconscious, I am not suggesting that this function is more important than the conscious. Both are of equal importance. But as in our culture it is the unconscious which has been devalued, it is necessary to redress the balance.

Whichever function is repressed, it will be projected through the anima and animus, most frequently onto one's partner. If women live wholly in accordance with their unconscious feelings, symbolized by their Moon, then they will project their inner power, symbolized by the Sun, onto their husbands. And inasmuch as men associate only with their conscious, rational sides, according to their Sun, so they will project their Moon onto their wives.

On a personal level, it is important to be in touch with our unconscious needs. Again I am stressing the unconscious because it is much easier to be out of touch with this side. And to be in touch with our unconscious means being open.

If we are open then we will recognize the signs that nature is constantly giving us. Nature never stops warning us when we are on the wrong track. It never ceases to re-direct us along the right path. But too often we miss these warnings because we fail to see their significance. We see, but we do not perceive. Then the warnings and signs get more potent – accidents, illness, marriage breakdown, until finally we get the message.

One such way is through our dreams. Jung, who had a great appreciation of their value, said:

> As the expression of an involuntary, unconscious psychic process beyond the control of the conscious mind (dreams) . . . show the inner truth and reality of the patient as it really is, not as I conjecture it to be, and not as he would like it to be, but AS IT IS.[1]

Just as the physical body automatically seeks what is best for it by a process of equilibrium in negative feed-back, for example in the control of body temperature and the regulation of blood-pressure, so the psyche also automatically seeks what is best. The unconscious 'knows' what is best for the psyche. The manifestation of the unconscious represents spontaneous attempts at self-regulation and the correction of errors through the events that occur in one's outer life or in one's dreams.

To get in touch with the unconscious, the conscious powers need to be used. The point, as I have stressed, is not a return to the womb, to the primitive state, but an acceptance of both functions. The conscious ego needs to relate to the unconscious in order to maintain adequate, healthy functioning. If we do not reach the unconscious knowingly, then its powers will be met in spite of ourselves.

As Whitmont has written:

> It follows, then, that what makes us ill need not be our worst, it may also be our best. But if the powers are not admitted, if doors and windows are barred, if it has to force its way in, a whole life may be damaged in the process.[2]

In order to understand the process of union of the psyche, it is useful to bear in mind the difference in the myth of Sumeria and that of the Bible. The aim of psychology as a healing process is to find, or rather to recognize, the wholeness or integrity of the personality. The mistake is commonly made that this means uniting the two halves into one.

This is not so. The aim is to accept both halves. To develop both sides equally, and to work towards a balance of the two opposing forces. The aim lies not in the achieving of such a balance for that would destroy the principle of duality which is the basis of life as we know it. The aim is in the path rather than in the goal, or rather the goal is the path.

Duality is a requisite of growth and it needs to be preserved. The aim is not perfection but containment, compensation through separateness. Not to get a mid-point, or to mix red and green into a dirty grey, but to juxtapose the two colours. The objective is to transform the opposing energies into a higher synthesis. Thus the two becomes the three – not the one.

Just as in a marriage between two people the goal is to develop the personality of each separately so that they can accept themselves and each other as individual people until a third principle is added, so in the marriage of consciousness and unconsciousness the principle of each is retained and a dialogue is established between the two.

The firmament holds the two apart. We need the conflict and the tension to provide the dynamic energy of life. As Jung has expressed it:

> Conscious and unconscious do not make a whole when one of them is suppressed and injured by the other. If they must contend, let it at least be a fair fight with equal rights on both sides. Both are aspects of life. Consciousness should defend its reason and protect itself, and the chaotic life of the unconscious should be given the chance of having its way too – as much of it as we can stand. This means open conflict and open collaboration at once. That, evidently, is the way human life should be. It is the old game of hammer and anvil: between them the patient iron is forced into an indestructible whole, an 'individual'. This, roughly, is what I mean by the individuation process.[3]

In the unconscious lie the archetypal forces, and it is these that we reach through to when we are in touch with the unconscious. It is these archetypal forces of nature that primitive man projected onto the constellations and which provide the fundamental symbolism in Astrology.

2 THE UNION OF MAN – PSYCHOLOGY, THE HEALING PROCESS

Be not another if thou canst be thyself.

PARACELSUS

Thus the aim of psychic healing, or psychology, is acceptance of the whole: conscious and unconscious together. It is containment rather than union. Acceptance of all that is within us. For everything that is contained within the psyche, taken together, is the Self.

How then do we attain completeness? It is necessary to distinguish containment from union. Union means that the two opposites become one. Containment means that out of the two a third factor is born. That is the essential difference. Jung has expressed the point thus: 'The point is not conversion into the opposite but conservation of previous values together with the recognition of their opposites. Naturally this means conflict and self-division.'

The error of the rationalist is that he cannot accept opposites or paradoxes. He insists in believing that there can be only one truth and that an entity cannot be more than one thing at the same time. The mystic knows that life is paradoxical. It is full of ambiguity. One thing changes into another and multiplicity is contained in unity.

Our very existence is based on duality and opposition. We can only see ourselves in a mirror. The reflection inherent in consciousness implies separation. Most of us only learn to see our characteristics by projecting them onto a partner through a relationship.

When God was one He was perfect. But He was not complete. The one had to become two so that God could see Himself face to face. God needs man as much as man needs God, for without man God could not participate in the life He created.

The principle of love, whether Divine or human, is one of union. But it is union by containment. In a sense it is necessary to lose oneself, to give up a part of oneself. But the losing is a transformation, not an extinction. The two parts are retained but transformed by each other so that a third force is produced. When two people love each other they do not become one in the sense of losing their individual identities.

When God showed His love for humanity and gave His only beloved son to mankind, He did not lose Himself. He created a third force, the Holy Spirit. Venus, the planet of love, is the union of the Sun and Saturn, the inner self and its shadow. From these two, from gold and lead, the Christ and Satan, love was born.

The regulative function of opposites was recognized by Heraclitus. He called this function *enantiodromia*. Sooner or later everything runs into its opposite. Winter inevitably turns into spring, autumn into winter. The reason why the beginning of winter was worshipped as the feast of Sol Invictus may at first appear obscure.

The first day of winter is the shortest of the year – the

darkest time, the nadir of life, the point of death. But just because it is the shortest day, so the days must get longer. The shorter nights are contained in their greatest length, the dawn begins to rise from out of the greatest darkness.

So the time of the Risen Sun was taken over as the feast of Christ's birth. And the Vernal Equinox, the beginning of spring and of new life, as the death of Christ. Birth and death, as opposites, are contained in each other.

> I have seen birth and death,
> But had thought they were different; this Birth was
> Hard and bitter agony for us, like Death, our death.
> T.S. ELIOT, 'Journey of the Magi'

The same principle is contained in Chinese thought. Ch'ien is Heaven, the creative, the positive force, and it is at the nadir of the day and the year. Just before midnight, before the Winter Solstice, when all is black. This time, the Chinese realized, was the time that the psyche, having reached the depths, could by its own creative effort, produce its greatest work.

K'un, on the contrary, is Earth. The midsummer, the calm, quiet heat of noon, the fecund period in the diurnal and annual cycle, the time of containment. In the fullness of life there is no spur to creativity, but peace and death in the long, hot, summer Sun.

Therefore the aim is to accept both sides. By accepting conscious and unconscious, by enduring the tension, we produce the energy for transformation. We endure the 'bitter agony' which seems like death, we sink to our lowest point, knowing that at that point, at the midnight hour, in the darkness of the night, the change must come. Then transformation takes place.

This is union for us. To accept the separation between conscious and unconscious. The first step is individuality. The second is individuation – the unity of the separate parts, the opposites. As Whitmont has said: 'When the dissociation between conscious and unconscious personalities is healed and redirected, individuality takes place; we become truly ourselves. This is the aim of therapy, and, it would seem, of life.'[4]

The function of analysis is to bring this about. To bring about, as Whitmont continues:

the change of conscious attitude, the metanoia. This is the indispensable prerequisite for the transformation, which itself, occurs spontaneously in the unconscious and cannot be brought about directly by any deliberate effort of will. (For) in transformation the DRIVE ITSELF becomes changed and ceases to trouble us, because it has turned its other face, has made a constructive and helpful impulse.[5]

Accepting all that is within us means consciously accepting those parts of ourselves that have either been pushed into our unconscious for one reason or another, or which have never emerged from our unconscious in the first place. This is the acceptance by the Ego, our conscious nature, of the Self, our whole being, including of course our unconscious.

As Anthony Storr has written:

The horrifying and primitive aspects of the psyche only remain horrifying and primitive if they are unrelated to the whole, and therefore unrelated to other people. The devil only remains devilish if he is dissociated from the deity from whom he took his origin.[6]

Unfortunately Hebrew-Christian religion as it came to be accepted encourages this very dissociation. Instead of accepting the whole, the Church has detached itself from nature by dispensing with the dark side of God. By maintaining that parts of us are evil in themselves, we have been induced to sever those parts, which effectively means trying to run away from aspects of our own nature.

Jesus, in his original message, laid great emphasis on acceptance of the whole. And until 600 A.D. Christ and Satan were accepted as equal brothers, the two children of God. The Sun and Saturn are both principles of the Ego, Saturn being the shadow of the Sun, and it is for this reason that in Babylonia Saturn was accepted as the ruler of the Sun. If we regard God as perfect then we reject parts of ourselves which we believe are sinful. Instead of accepting the shadow as an inevitable and necessary adjunct of the Sun, we project it onto others.

God should coincide with the archetype of the Self. He should encompass all, good and evil, everything in nature, and thus completeness rather than perfection. The shadow, the undeveloped, inferior, dark, 'evil' side needs to be recognized and accepted, for it is part of the whole, and to reject or destroy any part is to damage the whole.

In many ways we are worse off than our ancestors who worshipped the old gods. For the archetypal forces in the unconscious were externalized and projected into the forms of gods and demons and thus there was no temptation to identify them with their own ego. Now, instead of encountering the archetypes externally, they are encountered inwardly as the shadow or the Devil. That is why Astrology linked with psychotherapy, by recognizing the nature of these archetypal forces, can provide the ideal way of healing.

Life has an inner dynamism of its own. The amount of destructiveness is proportionate to the amount by which expansiveness is curtailed. We can see on the model of the Tree of Life how each archetypal force is balanced by another. Mars by Jupiter, Mercury by Venus. If one form of energy is thwarted, the energy that should be directed towards life is turned into destructiveness. And the more life is realized, the less is the drive towards destruction.

The aim is to reach the Self. The Self has been described by Jung as:

> A central point within the psyche, to which everything is related, by which everything is arranged, and which is itself a source of energy. The energy of the central point is manifested in the almost irresistible compulsion and urge to become what one is, just as every organism is driven to assume the form that is characteristic of its nature, no matter what the circumstances.

How is this aim achieved? In the first phase of life, the Ego needs to separate from the Self. Originally there is wholeness but it is an unconscious wholeness. The person is not an individual. He is still in the womb, or the walled garden of Paradise, happy in blissful ignorance.

In the second stage of life, the Ego is established and strengthened. Finally, when the Ego is developed, it can consciously return to the Self. Then, as an individual, a conscious encounter can be made. Then we return to the place whence we started and recognize it for the first time.

We become what we always were. We do not get anywhere on our journey through life. There is no goal; only the journey. The way and the way-goer are one. As Jung has said: 'The goal of psychic development is the self. There is no linear evolution; there is only a circumambulation of the self.'[7]

We are our Selves; we can be no other. It is in recognizing ourselves and being ourselves that we achieve wholeness. This does not mean doing nothing. On the contrary, it means finding our needs, facing ourselves, the unpleasant as well as the pleasant aspects of our nature, and transforming those parts we do not like into positive aspects of the whole.

If we are not our real selves, then we are at war with ourselves, and we will inevitably project this division onto the world outside. Carried too far, the internal division may break the psyche in two. 'Just as too wide a divergence from physiological equilibrium leads to discomfort, disease and death;' says Anthony Storr, 'so the attempt to be what one is not, or the failure to be what one is, leads to internal conflict, neurosis and emotional isolation.'[8]

The purpose of life then is to live one's own life. And it is important to get the order right. Here, as I have pointed out in a previous chapter, a common mistake is often made. Most people first decide what they want to do in life. They assert their aim and then they try to achieve it. This is the wrong way. First, we need to find our personal goal, our individual myth, and only then can we try to achieve it. This myth is contained in the Birth Chart.

Achieving this goal is not as easy as it may appear. However much they may assert the contrary, most people would do anything to avoid seeing their real selves.

First, we need to move away from that which we are not. As was said in the Greek Mysteries: 'Give up what thou hast, and then thou wilt receive.' We have to give up the facade we have erected. Then we need to move away from what we 'ought' to be, from the expectations of others. Then we can be open to experience and begin to accept ourselves.

As Carl Rogers has written:

> The individual moves towards BEING, knowingly and acceptingly, the process he inwardly and actually IS. He

moves away from being what he is not, from being a facade. He is not trying to be more than he is, with the attendant feelings of guilt or self-depreciation. He is increasingly listening to the deepest recesses of his physiological and emotional being, and finds himself increasingly willing to be, with greater accuracy and depth, that self which he most truly is.[9]

That self is our own individual myth. Each of us is unique and that is why we have to make the journey to find ourselves alone. We can be helped along our way, but ultimately the gate that we enter, or stand before, is ours and ours alone. Thus the aim of psychotherapy and Astrology can only be to help the client find himself.

Being oneself opens up a new way of living. Much of the therapy lies in the discovery of elements of ourselves that we are not aware of, aspects of the personality which the client had not recognized, and these factors are graphically portrayed in the Birth Chart. But being oneself does not only solve problems. We become more real because we come to recognize our uniqueness, but at the same time we are more alone.

The end of the journey has been described by Anthony Storr in the following words:

I propose to call this final achievement self-realisation, by which I mean the fullest possible expression in life of the innate potentialities of the individual, the realisation of his own uniqueness as a personality: and I also put forward the hypothesis that, consciously or unconsciously, every man is seeking this goal.[10]

3 FINDING THE SELF IN THE HOROSCOPE

That which we are, we shall teach, not voluntarily but involuntarily.

EMERSON

Astrology is the ideal method for discovering one's Self, for the whole Self is contained in the Horoscope. There, graphically portrayed, are all the parts that make up the whole. There, in the understanding of those factors, lies the promise of making oneself whole.

The advantage of Astrology over other methods of self-understanding is that it is the only system which displays the psyche of an individual in a symbolic way. No other system enables a therapist to see the whole person in this manner.

The aim of psychotherapy, as we have seen, is to put the patient in touch with himself. But simply looking at a Birth Chart will not put a person in touch with his Self. The patient, or client, must be helped to experience his complexes, his problems, his repressed energies, for himself.

It is often in the very effort of searching that he finds himself. The meaning and purpose of a problem lies not so much in its solution but in working at it incessantly. In this way the factors therein will be realized in the sense of being made real.

The owner of the Horoscope illustrated in Figure 2.1 needed to find his own individuality and free himself from the weak paternal-image he inherited from his own father. In coming under the influence of Freud, he projected the need for a father-figure onto the older man through his Sun-Neptune square.

When Saturn crossed his I.C. and Uranus passed over his Ascendant in 1913 he was brought face to face with the task of finding his own ego, finding effectively, the father within himself instead of looking for it outside. At that time, Jung broke with Freud, resigned as President of Congress and had a breakdown which lasted for three years. He needed that time to experience the meaning of these factors in his psyche.

No amount of rational explanation will bring the patient nearer to self-understanding. Astrology is a symbolic language and symbols are understood by the unconscious rather than by the conscious mind – intuitively rather than rationally. There is an old saying that when the pupil is ready, the teacher will come.

A person will come to an astrologer because unconsciously he knows of his problems. Then he is ready. Then the astrologer can explain the problems, he can bring the contents of the unconscious up into consciousness. Even if the client is not ready at that time, by leading him through the symbols, the truth will sink into his unconscious. Then, when he is ready, perhaps many years later, the seed will take root and it will come into consciousness. He may then remember the symbolism and thank the astrologer. He may believe that he has found the truth for himself. It will not matter. The astrologer's task will have been done.

Astrology is also a valuable tool for the therapist in order to help him to understand his client's psyche. However objective a trained therapist might be, it is often impossible to understand all his patient's problems. Jung said that on occasions he would look at a Horoscope to diagnose problems he could not otherwise see.

'Astrology consists of configurations symbolic of the collective unconscious which is the subject matter of psychology:' he wrote, 'the "planets" are the gods, symbols of the powers of the unconscious.' Each planet represents an archetypal force which is contained within each one of us. By looking at an individual's Birth Chart we can see how that particular force needs to be used by that individual.

Astrology provides the means of discovering the individual's myth. It is the personal path. Each Birth Chart is unique just as each person is unique. As we have seen, the Kabbalah together with the Tarot provide the means of understanding the universal myth. The Tree of Life is Universal Man, Adam Kadmon.

Before he looks at the individual patient, the doctor or surgeon needs a general knowledge of anatomy. He needs to understand how people as a whole function. He needs to know the connection of the liver with the spleen, the heart and the arteries. The astrologer, too, needs to relate the individual human being to the universal prototype.

That this is not appreciated by astrologers in the main is apparent from what most of them say in practice. Let us take the Moon as an example. The Sun-Moon polarity represents the main yang-yin forces within the psyche, conscious and unconscious. These two factors are as important as each other. They form an axis and in early times they were recognized as two faces of the same God.

Instead of recognizing this vital truth, astrologers have compounded the devaluation of the unconscious, feminine side of the psyche and thus of the yin factors in our culture. It has even been said that the Moon represents only the early environmental factors and that as the individual gets older he outgrows this part of his nature.

It should be clear from what we have already said on this subject, that such a suggestion is totally misleading. The Moon represents the unconscious and as such it symbolizes our inner needs. The Sun represents the conscious and our wants. Correlating one's needs with childish desires is psychically dangerous for it leads to the very repression of these needs that produces the problems we have discussed.

If we do not recognize these unconscious needs then we project them onto others and in particular onto our partners. That is why the Moon represents the anima and why many men unconsciously project their emotional side onto their wives.

Indeed it used to be said that the Moon represents a man's wife and the Sun a woman's husband. If we look for the principle behind these factors we can now see why that view was taken. The Moon symbolizes our feminine side and if we do not live out that vital part of our psyche, we will project it onto a partner. Inasmuch as a man attracts a wife through this part of himself, it will indeed represent his wife.

The same is true of the Sun. The Sun represents the inner power of consciousness, the Ego. If a woman does not live up to her own potential, then in turn she can project it onto a husband, and this was of course much more true in the times when there were few opportunities for women to apply their own potentials.

The Self is the whole Birth Chart, and by helping an individual to accept every part of his Birth Chart, the astrologer will be able to assist his clients to become whole people. There is a natural tendency to associate with only a part of one's Horoscope just as there is a tendency to associate with only a part of our psyches. 'I don't much like that Mars in Cancer square Neptune' but 'that's a beautiful trine between your Sun in Leo and Moon in Sagittarius'. That sort of approach is quite common, even though few would consciously admit it. It is the wrong approach.

First, everything in the Chart needs to be accepted. Second, there is nothing good or bad about any factor in a Chart. What matters is how it is used. Third, one cannot get away from the factors in the Chart. As we have seen, if we repress those parts we believe to be bad, then they become more powerful in the unconscious, rather than less.

Certainly some areas of a Horoscope will be more difficult than others. No one should pretend that Mars in Leo square Pluto is easy. But if it is a part of one's Chart, then one must understand it and come to terms with it. It is a part of that individual's nature and the only choice he has is to try to push it to one side or to transform it and accept it. He can rest assured, however, that it will pursue him doggedly and relentlessly until it is accepted or at least faced.

There is no running away from one's Self. If one refuses to accept one's own shadow, one will meet it continually in the street, in one's dreams, in one's secret fears. In the end we recognize that what we dread the most is our greatest friend. If we can bring ourselves to kiss the frog on the lips, we will transform its ugliness into beauty and its appearance will cease to trouble us.

We are bound to our Birth Charts as surely as Ixion was to his treadmill. We are born with these Charts. We die with these Charts. What then is the point? The point is that our Birth Charts have been given to each one of us for a specific purpose. There is all the difference in the world between having a Birth Chart and being one's Birth Chart. The latter implies conscious acceptance of what we are.

The difference between individuality and individuation lies in transformation. We are the same person at the end of the journey as at the beginning – but on a different level. We are spiritually reborn. We cannot change our Charts, but we can raise our level; we can attain a higher vibration by shifting the centre of personality from the Ego to the Self.

We can see this symbolically in the Horoscope. For the Ego is represented by the Sun, the circle with the dot in the centre. And the Self also is represented by the circle with the dot in the centre – but this is the whole Birth Chart. The symbol is the same but the latter encompasses the former, and contains all the factors that make up our psyches.

The Birth Chart is sometimes called a map. One needs to know one's path before one can follow it. One needs to know oneself before one can be oneself. 'Know thyself' was the inscription on the temple of Apollo. That is the opposite of trying to manipulate ourselves and others.

In providing man with his individual myth, Astrology gives meaning to the life of the individual. In connecting the general with the particular, it introduces a third factor. It links conscious and unconscious. The Sun, as Apollo, is the healing God whose power is to vitalize its maternal source, the Moon, who in turn contains and regenerates its potency and light.

CHAPTER 8
The fifth dimension

1 WHAT IS THE FIFTH DIMENSION?

How does the astrologer know on what level a factor in a Horoscope will manifest? A woman has Mars in her 7th House. What does this mean? Will she have a violent husband? Is she herself assertive in her relationships? Or does she need to be more assertive and does she also need the challenge of a strong partner to make her aware of this imbalance in her nature?

How does manifestation occur on the different levels? How can we be aware of and in touch with these levels? The astrologer cannot understand the meaning of the factors in the Horoscope unless he is both aware of and in touch with the different levels of reality. In order to be aware of these levels he must learn to see in the fifth dimension.

I have already described the four levels of existence in chapter 3. In order to simplify matters I shall now revert to just two levels. As I have pointed out, we cannot reach the spiritual level during our incarnation on Earth. What I shall for convenience call the spiritual level is in reality the higher mental or astral. The material level remains.

What then do I mean by seeing in the fifth dimension? At this point I should give a warning for it is all too easy to misunderstand this term. Indeed I might go so far as to say that one of the principle reasons for the failure to understand both reality in general and Astrology in particular is because of this misunderstanding.

What I mean by the fifth dimension is seeing the co-existence of unity and division. I mean seeing the whole and the parts as one and also as separate. I mean that in the fifth dimension 1 and 1 makes 3. Let me use a model to explain this for it is not easy to see in a new way.

The model I shall take is the mountain of Anki which I first mentioned in chapter 1. At the top of the mountain there is unity. This is the spiritual level. This is the abode of the gods – Heaven. On the Tree of Life it is equivalent to Kether. At the bottom of the mountain there is division. This is the material world where mortals live – Earth. On the Tree of Life it is Malkuth.

At the top there is eternity; at the bottom, time. At the top, the whole; at the bottom, the parts. At the top, the field, waves, the pattern; at the bottom, the separate particles. At the top, force; at the bottom, form.

And in addition to these two, there is the mountain as a whole. This is the vital point. That is why I said that 1 and 1 make 3. Seeing reality as a whole does not mean seeing only the whole in the sense of seeing only the top of the mountain. That is the fundamental fallacy which is so often made. Seeing reality as a whole means seeing the top and the bottom together.

The mistake that is so often made is to believe that reality exists either in the parts or in the whole, as if the two were mutually exclusive. We ask whether a factor in the natal Chart or a direction will manifest on the spiritual or the psychological or the mundane level. We ask if there is any intrinsic meaning in the separate factors in the Horoscope, whether the Moon in Taurus means anything in itself, or whether it is only the relationship of the factors to each other that contains meaning. We ask whether the correlation between the heavenly bodies and events on Earth is based on causation or synchronicity.

It is not a question of either/or. This is the assumption that has been made by those who can only see one thing at a time. It is the basis of Bertrand Russell's law of identity which incorporates that principle.

It is easy to think that everything is contained in the whole. For it is quite true that everything is contained in the whole. From the top of the mountain all is visible. But we can equally well see everything in the parts. The point is that both the top and the bottom are equally valid and equally real. And the second point is that both are the same – and yet different.

Heaven and Earth are the same. They are two aspects of one principle. God and Man are the same. Both were incorporated in the Christ. As the Son of God, His divine presence was manifested. As the Son of Man, His human aspect was revealed. We, too, are both human and divine. When we are in touch with our spiritual nature, we contact divine ground. When we align ourselves with our human nature, we function on the physical level. When we contain the two, we are in Tao, in a state of grace.

Heaven has its mundane aspect and Earth its divine. We can find the Kether of Malkuth and the Malkuth of Kether. There is a divinity in every aspect of life if we would but recognize it. And equally there is a physical aspect to everything in the heavens.

In the Horoscope of Jung (Figure 2.1) there is an exact square aspect between the Sun and Neptune. At the spiritual or archetypal level there is only potential; an innate force that may materialize on the mundane level in many different directions.

There may be great spiritual understanding, creative and artistic ability; sensitive, human insight; or an old man drunk under the embankment. As the sun breaks down, so might he. His ego may become inflated with visions of God, he might escape into an ivory tower, a solitary mister.

Both the potential and the manifestation are contained in the Horoscope's symbol. The separate levels blend into one, but in doing so they do not become extinguished. When exercising our free will to make choices the various manifestations of one potential become united but the separate strands remain to be invoked when our choice is made.

How then do we attain this fifth-dimensional viewpoint? First, two preliminary steps are necessary. We have to unlearn the old ways before we can recognize the new. We need to reach a state of unknowing where we are no longer governed by our preconceived notions and conditioning. And we need to be aware of the separate levels in themselves in order both to recognize them and to integrate them into ourselves.

But we cannot just see in a new way. We see partly because of our innate structure and partly because we have been taught to see in a certain way. There is a complex feed-back system between our minds and that which we perceive which governs the relationship between the two.

It has been said that things appear paradoxical because we see four-dimensional phenomena projected onto our three-dimensional senses. 'If we could visualise the four-dimensional space-time reality,' says Capra, 'there would be nothing paradoxical at all.'[1]

This is partly true but it is also misleading if taken too literally. First, what scientists term the fourth dimension is not equivalent to what I mean by the fifth dimension. As I pointed out in chapter 4, the scientist's concept of the fourth dimension does not embrace levels higher than the material. It merely adds time to space to produce what is in effect a linear space-time combination or continuum.

Second, the reason we do not see the higher dimensions is because we limit ourselves to the material level. If we see only with our physical senses then we can only function in three dimensions. A two-dimensional creature will be unable to see the three dimensions that exist in Figure 8.1. The further dimension is beyond its limited resources.

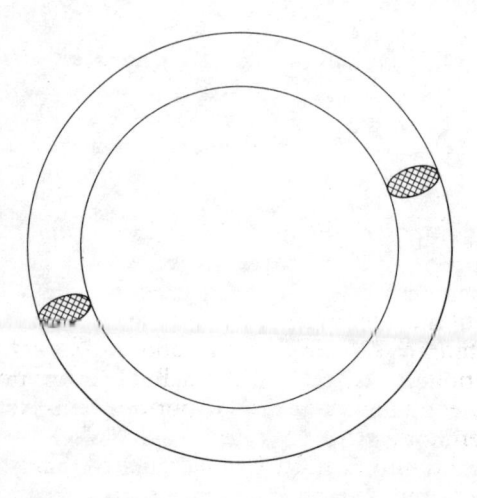

Figure 8.1 *A two-dimensional creature will see the two shaded areas as separate*

But the same is not true of us. The higher levels are present in each one of us. I have superimposed the five chakras onto the model of the Tree of Life in Figure 8.2. These five chakras are reflected in the sephiroth on the middle pillar. The fourth, which lies on the level of the throat, is equivalent to the invisible sephira named Daath beyond which we cannot pass in this incarnation. Yet the spiritual centre is contained within us even though we cannot reach it directly.

Thus the higher dimensions which exist in the universe are reflected in the centres that exist in us. The lowest level, the material, is where we normally function in three dimensions. The more nearly we are tuned into the higher centres, the more closely aligned shall we be with the higher levels in the universe of which we are a part.

2 THE WORLD'S ALMIGHTY MIND

> I'll sing how God the World's Almighty Mind
> Thro' All infus'd, and to that All confin'd,
> Directs the Parts, and with an equal Hand
> Supports the whole, enjoying his Command:
> How All agree, and how the Parts have made
> Strict Leagues, subsisting by each others Aid;
> How all by Reason move, because one Soul
> Lives in the Parts, diffusing thro' the whole.
> MARCUS MANILIUS

Einstein revolutionized science by equating matter with energy. Our understanding of energy is now about to be revolutionized by the equation of matter with spirit. But it is not only the two sides of the equation which are important; it is the nature of the equivalence itself.

Einstein's famous formula, $E = mc^2$, stated that matter could be converted into energy, and energy into matter. But the nature of the equivalence was based on the premise that matter and energy are separate. What we need to appreciate is that matter and energy are the same, and that matter and spirit are also the same.

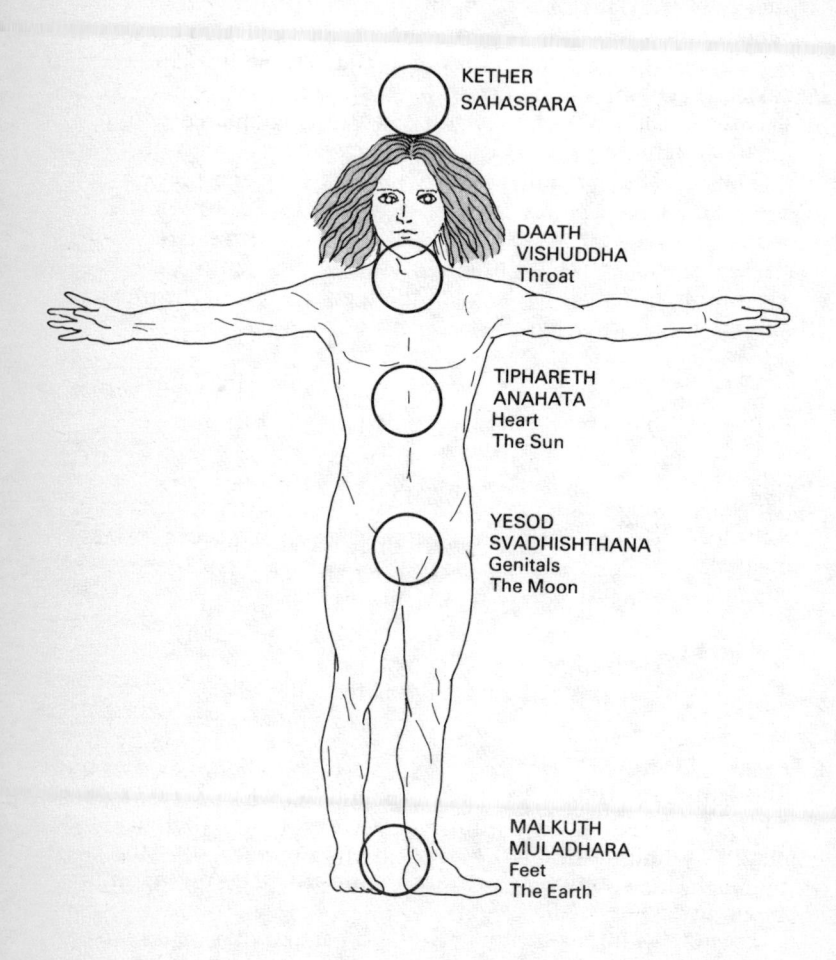

Figure 8.2 *The five Chakras on the Tree of Life*

The one is converted into the other because they are the same on different levels. One of the problems with scientific thought is that it has no model to incorporate the various levels that exist in the universe. That is why scientists have so far failed to resolve the material and the quantum levels.

Astrology, in the symbol of the Horoscope, does incorporate the two levels. But the symbol will not yield its inner truth unless it is perceived correctly. When we see in the fifth dimension, we see the two levels together, both as one and also as two. We see the whole and we see the parts.

At the centre, at the point, there is unity and stillness. At the circumference, there is motion, duality, change. But at the circumference there is also unity. The circle in its entirety is eternal. It is everlasting, without beginning or end. What it is to us, depends on our approach to it. We can stop its motion and examine a part of it, or we can become a part of it and be united with its wholeness.

The relationship between the parts and the whole, between time and eternity, between spirit, matter and energy is of particular importance in understanding the principles of Astrology for two reasons. First, because of the controversy concerning the separate factors in the Horoscope. Second, to enable us to decide if the correlation between the planetary bodies and events on earth is based on causation or synchronicity.

We have seen that there is a division among astrologers as to whether there is intrinsic meaning in the separate factors in the Horoscope. Does the Moon's position in Taurus in Figure 1.1 mean anything in itself? Or is its only validity contained in its relationship with the other factors in the Horoscope?

When we see in three dimensions we see the parts, we see material manifestation. We see the Moon in Taurus, we see Jupiter in Leo. We measure the distance along the ecliptic between the two separate factors and call it a square aspect.

We see Uranus 'out there' as a body in the sky. In 1913 it could be seen at 2 degrees of Aquarius, at the same point as the Rising degree in Figure 2.1. What then is the situation in these two cases? Are the Moon and Jupiter separate bodies or are they two parts of one whole? Is Uranus separate from the Rising degree in Figure 2.1?

Having in the past accepted only the separate parts, the tendency today is to go to the opposite extreme and embrace the whole while rejecting the parts. However, swinging the pendulum in the other direction as a natural reaction to scientific materialism, equally misses the point.

In itself it is perfectly right to appreciate the reality of the whole. Nor is this realization anything new. In the last century Hegel stated: 'Nothing is ultimately and completely real except the whole.'

More recently David Bohm has written:

> Parts are seen to be in immediate connection, in which their dynamic relationships depend in an irreducible way, on the state of the whole system (and, indeed, on that of broader systems in which they are contained, extending ultimately and in principle to the entire universe). Thus one is led to a new notion of *unbroken wholeness* which denies the classical idea of analysability of the world into separate and independently existing parts.[2]

The Holographic theory of mind and matter of Karl Pribram and David Bohm states that every part of the whole contains and implies the whole. Thus far, the theory is reasonable enough. It is important to see the whole in the parts and this is precisely what the astrologer does, or should do, when he looks at the moment of time which is symbolized in the Horoscope.

In a sense a part inevitably implies a whole. By definition a part must be a constituent of something greater than itself, otherwise it would itself be a whole. But just because it is an element of something else, and because that something else is real, does not mean that the parts themselves are not real. This is a conclusion that is easily, and wrongly, made.

The other fallacy in this Holographic theory is that it is based on determinism. To see the interconnectedness of every part, to see the reality of the whole, is both valid and useful. But to imply a sense of flawless structure into this whole, however aesthetically pleasing it may be, is neither logically necessary, nor correct.

It is the relationship between the parts and the whole which provides the solution to the riddle of reality. Let us look again at the E–P–R paradox with this relationship in mind. On the face of it, that experiment appeared to show that one particle could communicate with another instantaneously no matter how far apart the two might be. Bell's theorem seemed to corroborate that finding.

According to Einstein, communication which exceeds the speed of light is impossible because it infringes the laws of relativity. Yet telepathy happens. Precognition happens. The occultist finds nothing strange about telepathy or precognition because he knows that on the astral level the laws which govern time and space are different from those which operate on the material level.

The scientist too, if he accepts the quantum level, knows that its laws are different from those of the material level. There particles defy the laws of relativity, they appear out of the void, and disappear into the void again. On the quantum level the speed of light is reached, and exceeded. And on the astral level. For the quantum level and the astral level are two terms for the same phenomenon.

The material and the sub-atomic levels co-exist. Each is contained within the other. Similarly the physical and the astral levels co-exist, and each is contained in the other. At the material level there is diversity, there are the parts. At the sub-atomic and the astral there is the whole.

Pushed to the extreme, the physical world disappears. Everything turns into its opposite. When the physical world dissolves, the quantum level is reached, where each separate entity is part of the whole process. But the scientific mind, being unable to accept the resolution of the opposites, fails to see the relationship between the two.

In failing to understand the E–P–R paradox, the scientists have got stuck on the parts and have thus failed to see the whole. The assumption is made that there are two separate particles, and that therefore one must make a physical signal to the other. Similarly, in the two-slit experiment the assumption is made that because the particles always form a pattern, one must somehow tell the others where to go.

But the pattern which is formed by the particles in the two-slit experiment, the re-alignment which takes place by the particles in the E–P–R paradox, is not something separate from the particles themselves. Rather it is a question of looking at the same thing in a different way, of seeing in the fifth dimension instead of the third.

This should be apparent when we look at a black hole. We can see this phenomenon in one of two ways. At the centre all is stillness. In the middle of a black hole, time stops, the speed of light is reached. At that point there is limitlessness, infinity, eternity. So it appears to those who see the centre from the circumference. For those who reach the centre, there is no change. They remain a part of the stream of time and of life.

So too is the paradox of light resolved. Light is paradoxical, as we have seen, because light waves travel at a constant speed, 186,000 miles a second. This is the speed of the electro-magnetic spectrum which forms the underlying pattern of the universe. But although the waves travel at this constant speed, they interpenetrate the universe as a whole, and at the sub-atomic or astral level the speed of the waves appears to be exceeded.

We can look at these light waves in two different ways. We can see them separately or we can see them together. We can look at the particles, the photons, which make up the waves and see them travelling at 186,000 miles a second. In the search for the fundamental building block of the universe we find one electric wave made up of alternating positive and negative energy.

On the other hand, if we look at the waves as a whole, we no longer see movement. We just see the universe as a total pattern which exists simultaneously. Both ways of seeing the universe are valid. If we look at the interpenetration of the waves as a whole, at the total pattern, we see the astral or sub-atomic level. If we look at the separate waves or particles we see the material level. Each is as real as the other, and each is contained in the other.

Particles and waves, time and eternity, are not separate from each other. The waves are the pattern of the particles, eternity is the pattern of time. Thus duality resolves into unity. The difference between eternity and time, between unity and duality, is motion, or apparent motion.

Einstein had already shown in his relativity theories that (in

Capra's words) 'the activity of matter is the very essence of its being.' The world as we know it, on the material level, consists of activity and motion. If there was no motion, the material world would vanish. Whether it would cease to exist or merely become unmanifest is another matter. And again a matter of viewpoint.

On the sub-atomic or astral level there is unity. The particles in the E–P–R paradox and the two-slit experiment, which appear to be separate, are parts of the same totality, they are aspects of the same process. They do not move. The speed of light is not exceeded. It is just that the very recurrence of the waves produces the illusion, or the effect in causal terms, of movement.

It is we who break down unity into duality. We create the motion just as we have created our world. This in turn does not mean that duality is an illusion in an absolute sense. We break down unity and divide the world because we ourselves are divided. What we see in the outerworld is a reflection of ourselves.

The force of space and time is a unity. On this level the universe just is. It lies in wait in the stillness for us to introduce the concept of movement, separation and activity. The form differs. Although the speed of the waves is constant, the frequency varies. Each kind of matter responds to only one frequency according to the pattern of its constituent atoms, or according to their quantum value. In other words according to the numerical value of its individual energy pattern.

The principle of causation is based upon separation. One thing has a direct effect upon another. One particle makes its partner alter its direction. Another tells its fellow to go through the second hole rather than the first. A dying man makes a flock of birds settle on his windowsill. The Moon in Taurus makes a man slow-witted and pedantic. Uranus crossing his Ascendant makes his mind break down, and cuts the present off from his past.

The principle of synchronicity implies unity. Events happen because all things are aspects of the whole. The particles do not signal to each other. They are inextricably connected. The twin, whether it be a particle or a human being, does not need to send a physical message in time to its partner. There is an immediate connection between them that transcends time and space.

The dying man does not make the birds fly to his side. He and the birds are two forms of the same force that is present in the universe at that moment of time. The man born with his Moon in Taurus is a child of his time, the force of the Moon exists within him and without. In 1913 he dreams of a world in flames, millions of men destroyed in the conflagration of war, and Uranus passes by.

Let us look at a motor accident. A man leaves home, kisses his wife goodbye, drives quietly along the road to work. An ordinary day. In the country, on the route the man will take, a girl plays in the garden with her sister. The man drives through the town, heads towards the country lane. The girl throws the ball playfully over her sister's head. It bounces onto the road. Unaware, the man drives round the corner. The girl runs out across the road.

Suddenly, in that moment of time, two worlds collide. Two separate lives converge, united into one. Separate, that is, for the two participants in this 'accident'. There is no apparent connection between the man and the girl. Just as there is no apparent connection between the two shaded areas in Figure 8.1 for a two-dimensional creature.

We ask whether causation or synchronicity is at work. Was this collision caused by the man, or by the girl? Was it just an accident, something that just happened? I made the point earlier in this book that to get the correct answer, it is first necessary to ask the correct question. What then are we asking here?

We can see the same situation as an example of causation or synchronicity. If we want to explain a situation in material terms, to find out how an event occurs, we can look for a causative factor. If we want to know why something happens, if we want to discover the meaning behind the mundane phenomenon, we can look for a synchronistic element.

What we are really asking is: What is the nature of the connection between the two apparently separate constituents? As we have seen in chapter 5, according to Jung, things 'happen' to us in the world outside because we are not consciously aware of our inner needs. Then what is outside is attracted to us by what is inside.

Clearly neither the man nor the girl caused the collision by any deliberate act. Can one say, however, that the man caused the accident as a direct result of something within him, albeit something in his unconscious? Or did the girl attract the situation because of an unresolved inner need that could not otherwise manifest?

Jean Bolen has told the story[3] of a woman whose dog was hit by a car. This accident occurred just after her separation from the man she had been living with. Only once before had she owned a dog, and that dog was stolen immediately after she had made the decision not to marry the man she was then living with.

On the first occasion the dog was never found and the relationship had ended. On the second occasion both the relationship and the dog were still alive. Initially it was not certain whether the dog would live as its back had been injured, but it turned out that the spinal cord had not been severed. Ultimately both the dog and the relationship survived.

Jean Bolen describes these occurrences as examples of synchronicity. If one is looking for a physical explanation for what happened, it is perfectly valid to ask how these incidents were caused. If meaning is sought, if we want to know why these things happened, then it is not the event itself which is important, but the recognition of its inner purpose. Just as in the symbol, it is not the outer form that is important, but its inner truth.

The underlying unity or Tao connects everything in a given moment. It links the subjective element of the mind to the physical universe. There is the three dimensional world of cause and effect, where man and girl, woman and dog, are separate and apart. And the fifth dimension where spirit and body, inner and outer, are connected. Both dimensions are real. Both are contained in us. The question is which kind of reality do we want.

As Jung has said:

> The decisive question for man is: Are you related to something infinite or not? That is the criterion of his life. . . . Only consciousness of our narrow confinement in

the form of the self forms the link to the limitlessness of the unconscious. In this consciousness we experience ourselves concurrently as limited and eternal, as both the one and the other. In knowing ourselves to be unique in our personal combination – that is, ultimately limited – we possess also the capacity for becoming conscious of the infinite.[4]

3 THE WINGS OF THE MORNING – 5D ASTROLOGY

Wither shall I go from thy spirit? or wither shall I flee from thy presence?
If I ascend up into heaven, thou art there: if I make my bed in hell, behold, thou art there.
If I take the wings of the morning, and dwell in the uttermost parts of the sea;
Even there shall thy hand lead me, and thy right hand shall hold me.

Psalms 139.7-10

Let us then look at Astrology in the fifth dimension. Let us try to unite the two levels of spirit and matter, Heaven and Earth, and so understand the essence of the connection between the planets and our lives on Earth.

If we look at the universe from the top of the mountain, or from the centre of the circle, it is. The whole of it is contained in a total space time continuum. The past, present and future exist in potential. This is the universe in its spiritual state, at the Atziluth or archetypal level.

If we look at the universe from the bottom of the mountain, or from the circumference of the circle, it comes to life. Things happen. Events unfold. We have the choice of watching the drama like passive spectators, or of taking part in it when we give meaning to the events that happen to us. Ultimately the question that we are asked is whether we recognize the meaning of what occurs in our world.

The point of Astrology is to get in touch with the inner

meaning of the time. The universe describes itself in its parts. So the ancients looked at the flight of birds or the entrails of an ox because they recognized that every moment was its own and that by observing the phenomena in the world around them they could establish a connection with the pattern in the universe.

Everything that occurs in the universe reflects it at any particular moment of time. We can realize the quality of the moment simply by being, by being in tune with the universe, by being in Tao. We do not need Astrology any more than we need glasses to see. But Astrology can, and does, help us to experience the meaning of the universe, just as glasses can help us to see.

Most of us cannot experience this meaning directly and we therefore need to rely on the phenomena that reflect it. This is what Astrology provides so well. The quality of the universe is continually reflected in the planetary cycles, and we can find the meaning contained in the universe in these cycles.

The proviso is in the way we perceive the cycles. There lies the clue to the connection between the paths of the heavenly bodies and our lives on Earth. Astrology is descriptive. It is a more sophisticated method of description than the flight of birds because the paths of the planets can be plotted accurately into the future. But it must always be born in mind that there is no more point in the planetary cycles in themselves than in the flight of birds in themselves. They are equally an outward manifestation of an inner principle.

The archetypal principles can be seen by observing the movements of the heavenly bodies directly. These principles are worked out in their manifestation on Earth, in the daily events of our lives, on the mundane level. In order to integrate the different levels of existence, we need to recognize the descriptive nature of the universe.

Thus it is important to see the planets as part of a state of being as well as separate entities moving through space. We normally think of Mars as travelling through the sky at a certain speed, taking approximately two years to complete one orbit round the Sun. We can alter our frame of reference, and instead see the body we call Mars simply disturbing the space-time continuum, or rather being itself a disturbance of the space-time continuum.

Hence we can either perceive Mars as a physical object that is moving through the area of the sky we for convenience call Virgo. Or alternatively, we see that Mars is in Virgo. Looking at Mars passing through Virgo, we are in linear time. Seeing Mars in Virgo, we are in touch with eternity.

What of the woman with Mars in her 7th House? What is the meaning of this factor in this individual's Horoscope? If we see this lady the day after she has been attacked by her violent husband, do we say that she is not in touch with the right level? That she is unaware of her need to be assertive in her relationships? Or that she needs a violent husband?

Can we say that she has caused the violence that happened? Or that a principle within her psyche has synchronized with a part of the material universe which has reflected her need? Or that Mars in her Horoscope symbolizes both her need and its manifestation?

There is no either/or here. No one thing or the other. This lady has Mars in her 7th House. At the time she was born Mars was in a certain area of the sky. The position of Mars describes a principle both in the universe at that time and in she who was born the child of that time.

She needs to experience that principle. The principle in itself is valid; it is a factor in her psyche as it is in the universe. It is also a part of her whole being and needs to be seen in the context of her Horoscope as a whole, just as it is a part of the total pattern which was described in the universe at the moment of her birth.

If she is not consciously in touch with the principle symbolized by Mars, then it will rise up to meet her through the events that happen to her in her life. If she does not express the energy contained in that factor, then it will be projected and reflected in the world outside.

The principle needs to be understood. That much is obvious. What is of real importance is how that principle can be understood. All too often it is assumed that because the essence, or the spiritual level is sought, the material level is of no significance.

This is a mistake. The point in Astrology, as in life as a whole, is to understand the inner meaning of a principle through its material manifestation. That is what symbolism means – experiencing the spiritual level through the mundane event. Nor is it just a question of seeing through the materialization of the principle, and then casting it away like a worn-out shoe.

The real point, and one which is so frequently missed, is that in order to attain the spiritual level, we need to experience its manifestation at the physical level. For it is the physical level in itself that contains the spirit. The physical level itself is spiritual. It is not something separate. Spirit and matter are one and the same. Jesus in his human form was as divine as he was as the Son of God. Indeed the Son of Man and the Son of God were identical. There was only one Jesus – both God and man, and the same goes for each one of us and each form of life in the universe.

We talk about levels, we search for the spirit, without realizing that it is before us all the time. Teilhard de Chardin made the point so well in 'Le Milieu Divin': 'God is as pervasive and perceptible as the atmosphere in which we are bathed. He encompasses us on all sides, like the world itself. What prevents you, then, from enfolding Him in your arms? Only one thing; your inability *to see Him*.'[5]

And as de Chardin so eloquently stated in his writings, it is the ground itself which is divine. God is not 'out there', Truth is not 'out there'. It is contained in the events that continually happen to us in our lives, and in the people we continually attract. As we exist in this incarnation on the material level, it is inevitable that we should come to a realization of the principles in our psyches through mundane events.

A few perhaps will see the truth in a blinding flash of light. The mystic may reach the heights of ecstasy. For the rest of us, it is the goat's path that we must tread. Even St Paul suffered physical blindness for three days in order to reach enlightenment. The astrologer's task is to help people to love the ground on which they stand and to recognize and accept the factors in their Horoscopes.

The planets are symbolic in the same way that the flight of birds and the entrails of the ox and everything else in the universe is symbolic. But symbolism is not something separate from synchronicity or causation. It is a way of perceiving.

Because Mars symbolizes a certain energy in the Universe and in a lady's psyche, it does not detract from the synchronistic or causative nature of the events that manifest as a result of that energy. The flock of birds that landed on the windowsill symbolized death. It synchronized with an element in the dying man's psyche. It was attracted to him, caused by a factor in his unconscious, if one wishes to employ causative terminology.

The lady with Mars in her 7th House may lead a happy and fulfilled life. She may fight for the principles of justice and equality for her fellow human beings. She may be a great force for good in the world, helping the oppressed and those too weak or infirm to help themselves. She may instead rage inwardly against those who oppose her, constantly attracting antagonism and aggression.

It is easy to assume that the former is a 'positive' expression of the underlying principle, while the latter is a 'negative' expression of the same principle. In a sense that is true. But like most truths it is an over-simplification. There is no more need to look on a violent husband as a negative manifestation of that principle than there is to regard Christ's crucifixion as a negative manifestation of his life's work.

That woman may need a violent husband just as Christ needed to be crucified. She may not. When Jung broke from Freud, his mind broke down. Then, in his years of lonely agony, he became himself. He found the father he had sought outside, within himself. He needed to experience that principle in order to make it inwardly a part of himself.

What we need to achieve is to recognize the meaning in the material phenomena; whether it be the planetary positions or the flight of the birds, the motor accident, the theft of the dog or the violent husband. We can see the mundane and the spiritual in the same factor in the Horoscope. Sun square Neptune is both the alcoholic and the spiritual human being. And again, there is no either/or. The whisky priest may be a hopeless drunk and also a truly devout man.

Both levels occur in the same factor and through the same phenomenon. It is not a question of finding the spirit. We cannot escape from its presence. We find the spirit, the principle, what we need in our lives, by recognising and experiencing the spiritual essence of all that happens in the universe around us.

CHAPTER 9
Number – the pattern behind reality

All things are numbers

PYTHAGORAS

That number plays a vital role in the universe has been realized to a greater or lesser extent for millennia. The correlation between astronomy, music and mathematics which is based on number was appreciated by Pythagoras, Grosseteste, Kepler and Newton to name but a few. What has not been sufficiently appreciated, however, is either the full extent of the role that number plays, or the meaning of the numbers themselves.

One of the most exciting things about the scientific discoveries of this century, and one that will ultimately help to unite spirit and matter, is the realization that number forms the basis of the physical universe as we know it. What had hitherto been an intuitive insight on the part of the old scientists and mystics alike, has now become the cornerstone of the quantum revolution.

We shall look at number in the physical world in the first section of this chapter, and we shall there see that it is the principle that differentiates both one kind of physical reality from another and also the different levels, spirit and matter, Heaven and Earth, each one from the other.

As such number forms the pattern we call the universe. It is part of its warp and weft, and can be seen in the planetary cycles that reflect the structure of reality as we know it. At the time of birth, a pattern is created according to the numerical value of the universe at that moment.

That is one role of number. A role that is symbolic for it describes the quality of space and time. The other role, and one which has not been adequately recognized so far, is that of creator. Number is not only the pattern, and the means of differentiation. It is also that which creates that pattern, that which we call life, in the first place.

1 THE PILLARS OF THE TEMPLE – MANIFESTATION AND CHANGE

> Between heaven and earth there exists nothing but law and energy. The energy carries the law and the law regulates the energy. Law does not manifest itself; it is only through energy that the image yields the number.
>
> WANG FU-CHIH

What Wang Fu-Chih called the law is the pattern or structure that exists in the universe. Science has resolved the world into matter or mass and energy, and has discovered that both are the same. It is this mass-energy which forms itself into a pre-determined pattern. What then is the basis of this pattern?

The answer is number. The pattern itself, the law that lies between Heaven and Earth, is the level of Yetzirah in kabbalistic terms; the world of formation, the invisible stress system behind physical manifestations on the Assiah level. In scientific terms, this is the electromagnetic spectrum, the recurring pattern of waves which produces the form of physical matter.

As we saw in chapter 2, what has been called the quantum revolution provided two momentous insights into the nature of the physical universe. First, it introduced the concept of the freedom of matter on the particle level. Second, it showed that nature proceeds only according to the value of whole numbers.

Thus the only difference between one kind of matter and another, whether it be one chemical element, or one colour, whether it be a tree or a stone or you or me, is one of number. So the world is created in the form of number. This principle holds true whether matter is regarded as being made up of particles or waves.

In the former case, the electrons inside the atom have their orbits fixed by units of whole numbers and can only jump from one orbit to another in accordance with the value of those numbers. Such was the 'quantisized' model of the atom as put forward by Niels Bohr.

In the latter case, the waves that make up the electromagnetic spectrum can only exist according to the value of whole numbers. The waves themselves all travel at the same speed. What determines the type of manifestation is the amount of energy in these waves. And in turn the amount of energy is dependent on the frequency or the numerical value of the waves.[1]

Thus it is the rate of vibration, or frequency, which determines the differentiation between one type of manifestation and another. And it is the rate of vibration which also determines the level of manifestation. This too is the difference between mass and energy.

The higher the frequency, or the greater the rate of vibration, of the waves, the more energy is produced, and the less mass. Correspondingly the lower the frequency or vibration, the more mass is produced, and the less energy. For example, radio energy of extra low frequency vibrates only a few times a second, while gamma-rays have a frequency a billion times greater than that of visible light.[2]

Hence the material world consists of relatively motionless energy, while at the sub-atomic level where a higher vibration is reached, the material world dissolves. It is the rate of vibration that holds together the atoms and the molecules. If the rate is changed, so is the substance. As Capra has stated: 'Definite patterns arise in the atomic structure which are characterized by a set of integral "quantum" numbers and reflect the vibration patterns of the electron waves in their atomic orbits.'[3]

Here we can see how the underlying pattern is made manifest in a physical sense. The intrinsic pattern is contained in the reaction channels and manifestation depends on the amount of energy provided. The resonance, or unit of vibration, provides the energy of the colliding hadrons which is related to the frequency of the corresponding probability wave.

When the energy or frequency reaches a certain value, or number, the channel begins to resonate and then the underlying pattern is brought into being through sight or sound. In this way the underlying structure is contacted and by changing the rate of vibration the level of manifestation is altered.

We saw in chapter 2 that Walter Heisenberg was awarded the Nobel Prize for his matrix theory which reduced both particles and waves to the principle of number. Mathematicians, representing a purer or more abstract form of science than physicists, have tended to grasp the reality of numbers more readily than the latter.

In the circumstances it should come as no surprise that Heisenberg's insight was not more readily accepted among his colleagues. Particles and waves are convenient models for what happens inside the atom and in the world at large and in this sense they are symbolic. What should not be lost sight of is that the principle which is symbolized by both and which resolves the two, is number.

When the rate of vibration is raised, the material world disappears. It is at this point that we can combine the worlds of the scientist, the occultist and the psychologist and see that their respective models all describe the same underlying reality. The energy field of the scientist or the entire electromagnetic spectrum is the astral plane of the occultist and the Collective Unconscious of the psychologist.

As the frequency is increased, so we reach more nearly towards the spiritual level. At this level, there is pure energy. Here, where the universe simply is, there is complete freedom and absolute determinism, total chaos and the entire law. For here all is potential: all possibilities are contained in its unity.

The lower the level, the less freedom exists, and therefore the more will is necessary to produce change. At the lowest, material level we are bound by our physical bodies and the relatively inflexible laws of material existence. At the intermediate level of the sub-atomic and the astral, in the formative world of the imagination and dreams, there is more freedom at our disposal.

Differentiation between the sub-atomic and the material level occurs spontaneously. Hadrons appear out of the void and vanish again in quantum physics. Differentiation between the astral and the physical, and between the unconscious and the conscious, can occur either spontaneously or deliberately. In all three cases, the underlying pattern remains. It is only the rate of vibration that changes.

The occultist uses the power of vibration through the resonance of sound to alter the levels and bring down from the astral to the physical. This is the basis of the power of the word in magic and the creation myths which have brought the world into being.

Here too we see number in its second role, that of creator, as well as created. Evolution, or creation, consists of the spontaneous formation of numbers from their own source. I shall discuss these two separate roles of number in the next section of this chapter.

At this stage, it needs to be appreciated that the form occurs as the result of the combination of the frequency of the vibration and the nature of the material being vibrated and that the difference in both depends upon the value of the underlying number.

The resonance first affects the intermediate level, the astral or electromagnetic spectrum or energy field, and it is then reflected on the material level. The relationship of the material form to the rate of vibration was originally discovered by an eighteenth century German physicist, whose patterns in the sand which resulted from notes played on a violin, have been named Chladni figures.

That original discovery was later refined by Hans Jenny whose theory of 'Cymatics' was based on the invention of a tonoscope which converted the vibrations of the human voice into shapes. Thus the resonance contained in the vibration produces the force which in turn brings into being or changes the form.

2 THE DUAL ROLE OF NUMBER

There is a mysterious connection between Gods and numbers.
                                                    PYTHAGORAS

When talking of numbers, even a materialist like Bertrand Russell can wax lyrical: 'Mathematical objects, such as numbers, if real at all, are eternal and not in time. Such eternal objects can be conceived as God's thoughts.'

Numbers are symbolic but to conclude that they are, therefore, unreal is to fail to appreciate that the universe in which we live is itself symbolic. In this section I shall examine the dual role of number, as both creator and created, and also the underlying meaning of numbers which in turn can only be properly understood if both functions are appreciated.

We have seen number as change, as differentiation, in the levels of existence and in the difference between one object and another. The pattern of the universe, on whatever level, is simply number, whether we count the number of electrons in an atom, or the value of their ratios, whether we look at the vibrations in the waves or listen to the unceasing beats that make up the harmony of the spheres.

How did the pattern come into being in the first place? Here too we find that the answer is number. Life as we now know it, the multitudinous, incredibly complicated pattern that is number, was itself created from its own origin.

As soon as the one divides into the 2, a relationship between the two of them is created by the very fact that there are two instead of one. When the 3 is generated from the 2, then a new pattern is formed. Thus the pattern which now forms the universe is inherent in the numbers themselves and is created by the numbers.

Numbers are both quantative and qualitative. That is to say they are both potencies, or principles, and they are also relative. These are the two roles of number and it is vital to distinguish between them.

Therefore, on the one hand they represent universal principles and in this sense they are archetypes. On the other hand they are part of a process which evolves from unity to diversity, from the 1 to the many. In this sense they are relative and they obtain their meaning from their relationship.

This appreciation should help to understand the confusion which has risen over the meaning of the numbers. This is first, because the emphasis has been placed too much on their relative nature. The 5, for example, is thought of simply as a combination of the 2 and the 3, or of the 4 and the 1. This is correct as far as it goes. But in addition to its relative meaning, the 5 is also a principle in its own right.

Secondly, there can be no absolute meaning to the numbers just because they are relative. All the lower numbers derive their meaning from the higher ones and they need to be understood in their relationship to those that precede them. And an element of paradox is introduced where the meanings of the numbers are reversed according to their different levels.

The principle of force, for example, can be seen in the 2, and thus form in the 3. In this sense form is a pattern but it is not manifest form in the shape of a tangible object. Thus form as a pattern is the 3 and the tangible manifestation of that abstract pattern is the 4.

It is especially important to distinguish the two separate uses of number in Astrology. The first use, or series, which we can for convenience call 'Primary Numbers' incorporate the underlying principles of number. The 'Secondary Numbers' describe the alternating current of positive and negative force and thus the relationship between the 'Primary' series.

These two functions of number are contained in the sephiroth on the Tree of Life. Each sephira, corresponding to the numbers from 1 to 10, is a potency or principle in its own right. And each number creates those succeeding it and thus the latter flow from the former and partake of their nature.

This is not creativity in any deliberate sense but a principle that is itself inherent in the essence of the creator. Creation is evolution in the sense that it is a continual process. Thus if there are two, then from those two a third force will evolve: love from two human beings, a book or work of art from an individual and his or her material.

Creation itself is a process and a paradox. Russell as a materialist stated that numbers are eternal and not in time. In one sense this is true. Meister Eckhart has said: 'There is no number in eternity, it transcends number.'[4] So it does, but it also creates it.

As the Tao Tê Ching points out: 'Tao gave birth to the one, the one gave birth to the two, and the two gave birth to the three, and the three gave birth to all things.'

Eternity is 0 – nought, nothing, the circle. But how we see the circle depends on us, as I have previously stated. It is nothing and everything. It contains all within itself. It is potential. As the unmanifest, it is nothing. As spirit, it is everything. If we travel round it, it is the circumference, the wheel of life that all mortals must tread. Then it moves and we move with it. If we see it as a whole, it is eternal and we partake of its spirit.

From the 0, from the Void, is formed the creator, the 1, the dot in the circle. This is God the Absolute, Kether, created from the Ain Soph, finite with respect to Negative Existence, and infinite with respect to Positive Existence.

When the dot, as God the creator, moves there is action and time. When He is still there is non-motion, the Absolute, which also includes time. This is the paradox which Russell, basing his thought on the so-called law of identity, could not appreciate.

It is also the paradox of light. Light moves at a constant speed but if one is moving at that speed, then one is not moving. This too is the basis of light as the creative principle, of God as the spirit of light and life.

The 1 then is the point, eternity, lack of movement. The 2 is the line, the principle of difference, of duality. The 1 is God Himself. The 2, God looking at Himself, becoming aware of His own nature, His reflection. The dynamic principle, the rod of power or wand, a channel for a passage of force which can be seen in the two hands of the Magician, himself number 1, which point up to Heaven and down to Earth.

In psychological terms, it is the beginning of relationships. The chance to become more of an individual by relating to another. In the words of Martin Buber: 'Through the Thou a man becomes I.'[5]

Three is the underlying pattern, the arrangement, the form enclosed in the triangle. Stability, the discipline of force. Four is the form, as we have seen, on a tangible basis. For the first three numbers form the Supernal Triangle on the Tree of Life. These we cannot reach in this incarnation, they are the abode of the spirit.

It is only when we reach the 4 that we get manifestation on the physical level, although even this is far above the terrestrial level which is only attained fully in the number 10. The 4 then is the formation of the abstract idea, and in the four directions of the cross are seen the four elements in equilibrium.

Then in the 5 we have the release of force in Activity and therefore Man. These then are the underlying principles of number in the context of Astrology.

3 THE NUMBER OF THE STARS – NUMBER IN ASTROLOGY

> He telleth the number of the stars; and calleth them all by their names.
>
> Psalms 147.1

We have seen that the principle of number operates in two separate ways. The force that creates the pattern we call the universe is number, and the creation that is the pattern of the universe is also number. The creative force is contained in the planets themselves. They are the potencies that weave the fabric of life and of the world.

That life, and the world which contains it, emanates from the relationship that is formed by the planetary forces. It is brought into being, into the differentiation of manifestation, by the planetary aspects, the contacts they make with each other, both in the pattern that is the Horoscope at the moment of birth, and in the later contacts that are made from that moment on.

The planets themselves, as potencies or gods, get their meaning from the number of their spheres as they rotate round the Earth. This is, of course, from our viewpoint as it is that viewpoint which provides meaning for us and thus to our reality.

In this sense it does not matter whether the planets exist in a physical sense or not. They are symbolic as all life is symbolic. It is their motion in the space-time continuum, or their existence as part of the space-time continuum, alone that matters.

Because the planets get their meaning from their orbits, their numbers are necessarily dependent upon these orbits. Thus we can see in Figure 9.1 how the numbers correspond to the planets. This is also the order of the planets on the Tree of Life and that incorporated in the planetary hours, as viewed from the Earth.

It is worth emphasizing at this point that although the importance of numbers is generally accepted, one of the major practical problems in Astrology and in numerology has been the correspondence with the planetary forces. If we accept that it is their orbits as viewed from the Earth which gives meaning to the planets, then we can understand the true basis of the correlation.

NUMBER – THE PATTERN BEHIND REALITY

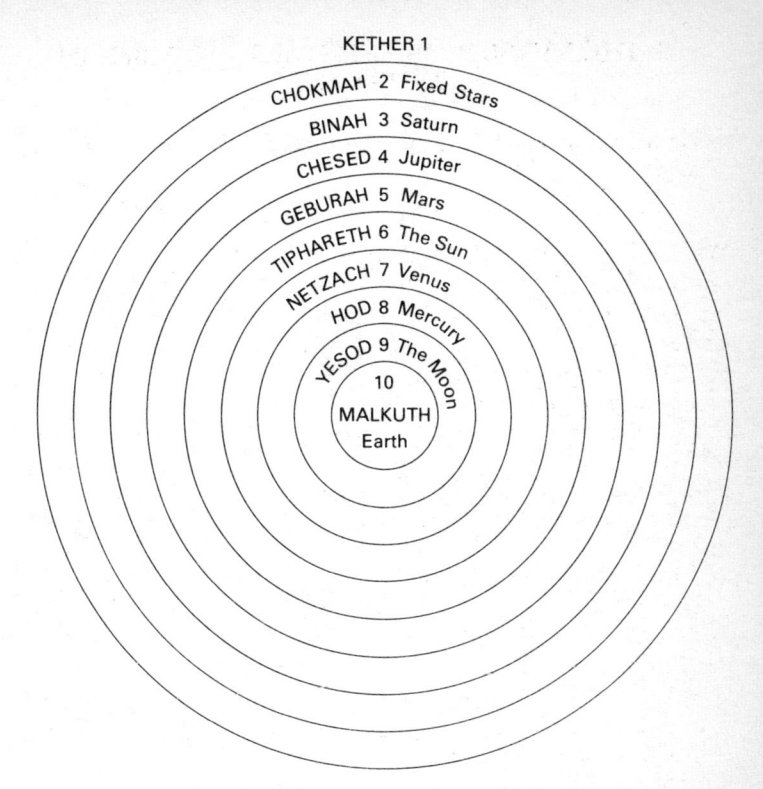

```
            KETHER 1
       CHOKMAH 2 Fixed Stars
         BINAH 3 Saturn
         CHESED 4 Jupiter
         GEBURAH 5 Mars
         TIPHARETH 6 The Sun
          NETZACH 7 Venus
           HOD 8 Mercury
           YESOD 9 The Moon
               10
            MALKUTH
              Earth
```

Figure 9.1 *Correspondence between numbers and the planetary orbits*

The potency of the planets depends on the value of their numbers. The planets which are further out are more powerful in their effects, while those which are nearer are more potent in themselves as archetypal principles. The smaller numbers represent the basic principles that are operative in the universe. As we proceed from unity to multiplicity so we leave the basic principles and begin to diversify into more complicated forms of life.

As the planets continue to move in their orbits, passing through different areas of space-time, so they describe more and more complicated patterns. Their relationship with the

Signs, the areas of the sky through which they pass and of which they are a part, with the Houses, their interaction with the Earth's rotation, and with the aspects, their relationship with each other, describe the patterns which continually come into being at each moment of time.

In their interaction, as a result simply of their motion which in turn is an integral part of their being, we see the second role of number. The first role is the number inherent in the planet itself according to Figure 9.1. This is the quality or descriptive value of the number and is equivalent to the 'Primary' series I mentioned in section 2 of this chapter.

The second role is the value of the number which is inherent in the aspect or relationship that the planets make to each other. Thus the conjunction is 1 or unity, the opposition 2 or duality, the trine is 3, the square 4, the quintile 5, the sextile 6 and so on, according to the division of the circle.

As we have noted it is the second function of number which has been generally recognized in Astrology to the detriment of the first, which can be seen in the modern tendency of seeing the aspects alone as representing the principle of the numbers. Indeed the tendency has been carried so far in certain cases that the inherent meaning of the Signs and Houses is almost lost.

But the areas of the space-time continuum we call the Signs and the division of the Earth's motion we call the Houses have themselves been created according to the inherent value of the numerical frequencies that emanated from the planetary principles according to the human mind.

The energy field of the physicist is equivalent to the aura of all living organisms. The reason why certain areas of the sky have certain characteristics, why the Signs of the Zodiac are real, is because their energy field or aura has been imbued with the traits of the archetypal myths by projection from group minds throughout the ages.

And the reason why we have two different Zodiacs, the tropical and the sidereal, is because two different cultures have projected their own telesmatic images onto the same area of the sky. Thus meaning is contained in both according to the ability of the individual to tune into the underlying principles.

We should now be able to see a Horoscope in terms of fundamental reality, simply as number. As the universe vibrates to the value of certain numbers, so the universe will describe a specific numerical pattern at any moment in time. The particular moment in time that is symbolized in the Horoscope as the birth of an individual is therefore the pattern of number that is described or created at that time.

That is why the Horoscope is described by a moment in time. The individual born at that time will always vibrate to the pattern of resonances that is inherent in that time. Thus our individual space-time is the universe's space-time at that particular moment. There is just the universe and we are a part of it.

The natal planets in the individual's Horoscope will therefore always describe a disturbance in the space-time continuum throughout all time. Because the factors in the sky at the individual's time of birth describe his particular pattern or vibration, we can see that he will always respond to that vibration, both before and after his birth. Thus the future is laid down for all time at the moment of birth and all time is eternally present.

By seeing the planets and life as a whole in terms of number we can understand for the first time how future directions work. A differentiation has been made between transits which describe the actual positions of the planets in relation to the Horoscope at any particular time and the so-called 'symbolic' directions, for example secondary progressions and the 'one-degree' method which are based on the principle that one day is equal to one year.[6] We can now also appreciate that these two apparently different types of directions are based on the same principle.

Let us look at transits first. What the astrologer says here, as we saw in chapter 1, is that because the person whose Horoscope is illustrated in Figure 1.1 was born when the Sun was in the area of the sky we call 22 degrees of Cancer, he will be affected in some way whenever another planet passes either over that degree of the ecliptic or is at a specific distance from that degree, even though the Sun is no longer there.

Clearly, therefore, it is not this person's Sun itself which is being affected, but the area of the sky where the Sun was placed at the time of his birth. And the way that the transiting planets affect that area of the sky is in two ways, which is dependent on the two different ways that numbers function.

The Birth Chart has a particular natural frequency which can be seen in the positions of the natal planets, and in the value of the numbers of those natal planets according to the Primary Series. These planetary vibrations, or numbers, are then acted upon by the alternating force of transits which coincide with the natural frequency contained in the individual's Birth Chart.

This is precisely how form is brought into manifestation on the physical level by the interaction of a vibrating current on the underlying material as we have seen earlier in this chapter.

Thus the meaning of a particular number is brought into manifestation, the number 4 in the square aspect, for example. The fact that the natal planets are not in the sky at the time does not matter for it is a question of the relationship between the transiting planet and the vibration in the individual.

Because of the planetary positions in the Birth Chart, the individual vibrates at a particular rate, he is on a certain wavelength. This is the individual pattern, and it is with this that the transiting planet harmonizes according to its own vibration or number value.

This is what happens when Saturn transits an individual's natal Venus. When, for example, Saturn is at 27 degrees of Capricorn in January 1991, Saturn will then vibrate with the owner of the Horoscope in Figure 1.1 according to the quality of Saturn's integral number, i.e. the number 3, and secondly, according to the quality of its aspect, i.e. the number 2.

According to the 'symbolic' directions one day, or one degree, is equivalent to one year, or sometimes to one month. What is actually happening in these cases? I shall look for this purpose at secondary progressions where the actual positions of the planets so many days after birth is equivalent to the same number of years after birth, and at the 'one-degree' method where each degree is equivalent to one year in the individual's life.

Here again we find the answer in the value of the numbers. It is the particular part of the space-time continuum that is being contacted in all these cases. A day, a month, a year are equivalent because when the Earth, the Moon and the Sun revolve according to their respective motions in a day, a month and a year, they contact the same part of the space-time continuum.

If we look at the Sun's apparent movement around the ecliptic and compare it with the Earth's, we can see that the Sun will pass through precisely the same parts of the ecliptic in one year as the Earth will in one day, and that the Moon will in one month.

Thus if in the natal Horoscope Saturn is at 1 degree of Scorpio and the Sun is at 8 degrees, in seven years the Sun will have passed over the position of Saturn and the Sun seven times, and in seven months the Moon will have passed over those positions seven times, while in seven days the Earth will equally have passed through those degrees seven times.

In the 'one-degree' system the Sun will have passed over the particular areas as many times as there are degrees apart. Time is cyclic, and the pattern re-appears and coincides. Any later contact coincides with the original pattern, with its resonance, to produce the harmony of the spheres. Thus transits, progressions and the other directions, all describe our later condition at any future time.

If we are to be in touch with our inner natures which are symbolized in our Horoscopes, we must learn to respond to the planetary vibrations which reflect the archetypal forces both in the universe and in ourselves. How then can we assimilate the meaning of these forces?

We, like the rest of the universe of which we are a part, are made up of the archetypal energies which are contained in the symbolism of number. Just as the different levels are already in us through the Chakras, so are the planetary energies which can also be seen in their ideal form on the Tree of Life, and in their individual alignment in the Horoscope. Here too we can see why it is essential to accept Astrology and the Kabbalah as integral parts of one system.

In the ancient religion of Mithra, neophytes had to go through an initiation ceremony, the aim of which was to incorporate the various planetary energies. The orbits of the Sun and Moon and the five planets were conceived as layers round the earth through which the soul descended when it came to be born.

These seven layers correspond to the seven rays which make up the human aura. After birth, the individual had to assimilate each planetary ray or zone so that he finally reached an unqualified or integrated state where he could function on all levels. In this way all the different kinds of space-time frames were made a part of him.

We can see in Table 9.1 the seven degrees of initiation. When we compare these with the planetary energies and their corresponding numbers we see the same sequence that governs the numerical value of the planets.

Table 9.1 *The seven degrees of initiation and their correlation with the planets and numbers*

The seven degrees of initiation of Mythra		Planets	Numbers
Corax	Raven	Saturn	3
Cryphius	Occult	Jupiter	4
Miles	Soldier	Mars	5
Leo	Lion	Sun	6
Perses	Persian	Venus	7
Heliodromus	Runner of the Sun	Mercury	8
Pater	Father	Moon	9

Once these planetary vibrations have been assimilated we achieve the power to consciously change the level of our lives. We can tune into ourselves, into our various centres, and we can tune into the universe and the rest of nature and align ourselves with its power.

That this is our quest is embodied in an old kabbalist story telling how the child is formed by God and sent into the world. God says to the soul of the child:

'The world to which I send thee is better than the world in which thou wast; and when I formed thee, I formed thee for this earthly fate.' Thereupon God orders the angel in charge of the souls living in the Beyond to initiate this soul into all the mysteries of that other world, through Paradise and Hell. In such manner the soul experiences all the secrets of the Beyond. At the moment of birth, however, when the soul comes to earth, the angel extinguishes the light of knowledge burning above it, and the soul, enclosed in its earthly envelope, enters this world, having forgotten its lofty wisdom, but always seeking to regain it.[7]

CHAPTER 10
The union of Heaven and Earth

1 THE CENTRE OF THE CIRCLE – THE CORRELATION BETWEEN INNER AND OUTER

> The stream of creation and dissolution never stops. . . . All things come out of the one, and the one out of all things.
>
> HERACLITUS

We have travelled round the circle seeking explanation and meaning. Now we return to the place where we started. What is the correlation between the heavenly bodies, the planets in the sky 'out there' on the one hand, and events on Earth and the human psyche on the other? And what is the meaning of this correlation?

The reason for the correlation between outer and inner is very simple. Both are the same. The reason for our inability to see this is equally simple. We are divided. Therefore we inevitably see the world as divided. We see the planets 'out there', moving through the sky and we see things happen on Earth.

Unfortunately the simplicity ends there. Truth by its very nature is simple. Understanding the truth is, on the contrary, far from simple. The truth is the whole, and the problem that we face is how we, who are a part of that whole, can see the unity which contains us. We are, as it were, inside the circle, searching for a vantage point whence we can look in.

This is why it is often more easy to understand by means of the direct experience contained in parable or poetry than in the verbal speculation of philosophy. The point was aptly made by Sir Philip Sidney in his *Apology for Poetry*:

> (the philosopher) teacheth, but he teacheth obscurely, so as the learned only can understand him, that is to say, he

teacheth them that are already taught. (But the poet is) the right popular philosopher (who) yieldeth to the powers of the mind an image of what whereof the philosopher bestoweth but a wordish description; which doth neither strike, pierce, nor possess the sight of the soul as much as the other doth.[1]

What we do in practice, in our search for truth, is to keep pushing back the doors. We start with the material level, we observe the world 'out there', then we delve deeper into the quantum or the astral level. At the next stage we reach the underlying stress system of the world, the energy field, the electromagnetic spectrum, the pattern behind the world of form. This we resolve into an even purer principle – that of number.

Even at this stage, we have not reached the end of our journey. There is still one, final step to take before we reach the Absolute. That step we shall now take. But before we take it, we must realize just what it is that we are trying to find in our search for truth.

If we want to find the truth, then it is valid and necessary to keep pushing back the doors towards the Absolute. The mistake, however, is to believe that the truth is contained any more in the Absolute than in the intermediate stages.

Each step along the way contains the truth. Our journey is round the circle. Each part of that circle is real. At the end of the journey we arrive where we started. We go round in circles. But going round in circles does not mean that we learn nothing. Whether or not we learn anything along the way depends on us. The point is that it is the journey itself that contains meaning. The goal is the travelling, it is the experience of everything that we meet in our search, not just in what faces us when we reach our journey's end.

The fallacy is to believe that the purer the truth, the more real it is. On the contrary, when we reach the Absolute, the truth is simply more pure. No more, no less. It is no more true. All the levels are real. They all co-exist – the material, the astral, the higher mental, the spiritual. Or in scientific terms, the physical, the quantum, the electromagnetic spectrum, the space-time continuum.

We need to reach the Absolute, but we also need to realize that the Absolute is the beginning of the journey, not the end. Here we reach the void. At this point, the material world does not disappear. It is not, as many scientists believe, an illusion. On the contrary, everything is contained in the void, in the Absolute. We start with the material level, at Malkuth, number 10. As we progress up towards greater purity and unity, we finally reach the 0. Then the whole Tree, all the numbers that symbolize the archetypal energies of existence, should be integrated within us. Then all the levels of reality should co-exist in our nature.

It is all too easy to think that this is the end. Having travelled round the circle, what have we gained? Nothing. We are left with nothing but the circle – which itself is the 0. But this is the whole point. In the words of the Buddha: 'I obtained not the least thing from unexcelled, complete awakening and for this very reason it is called "unexcelled, complete awakening."'

We need to reach the level of unity in order to appreciate that the universe is a whole. The universe simply is. Because we are divided, we break down this unity into what we perceive as the material world. We separate inner from outer. We create the parts according to our own nature.

But the parts, and the material world of which they are made up, are no less real because they have been created by us. First of all, they are not created out of nothing. They are created in the same way that we are created. Second, they are real for us just because they have been created by us.

We have reached the stage where there is both structure and chaos, order and change. At the material level, there appears to be structure. We can look at the past and predict the future with reasonable certainty; we can see that a specific event occurs as a result of a particular action.

At the lower levels, there appears to be chaos. We cannot tell what an individual sub-atomic particle will do. We cannot tell what Mrs Jones will do when transiting Uranus opposes her Venus. And yet if we look at the individuals as a whole, we can see a pattern. We can see that however the individual particles, or human beings, behave, they appear to group themselves into a structure which is predetermined.

And we have seen that this pattern, or underlying structure in the universe, is based on number. The whole world, and the whole of life as we know it, is arranged on the principle of number. The planetary motions, the differentiation between one form of life and another, the archetypal energies that determine our reactions to the world around us, all are founded on the axiom of number.

However, having said this, having apparently accepted the principle of structure in the universe, having provided us with a sense of security and order, we must now pull the rug from under our feet. Inasmuch as every level is real, and inasmuch as there is structure on the material level, then this structure is real.

But it is not real in an absolute sense, for we have not yet reached the Absolute. What is this structure that I have apparently accepted, and that many theorists have so gladly, but blindly, embraced? Why is it only the penultimate level?

The reason is that this apparent structure is only the way that we, as humans, perceive or react to the chaos or the void. The final level is the void, chaos. There is nothing else. This is the Absolute. Thus the world was created out of chaos and, at its primal level, it remains simply as chaos.

This is a conclusion that is not easily accepted because it suggests that we do not exist. And therefore it is natural to look for something safe on which to cling, to seek out structure and order in the universe, so that we should not fall into the abyss. But this is precisely what we need to do. For it is only when we reach this ultimate level that we can begin to recognize the reality of each level in turn. Only in this way, by having the courage to lose ourselves, can we lose the fear of fear itself.

Accepting chaos as the ultimate level, does not mean that there is no structure in the universe. Just because we create this structure, does not make it any the less real. I have said that life 'as we know it' is based on the principle of number. This is the clue. It is our life and our world which is real for us.

The materialist thinks that because we create the world with our minds it cannot be real. That is why many scientists today have come to the conclusion that the universe is an illusion, that it is maya. The flaw in this viewpoint is that we do not create the world out of nothing. We ourselves are created in a certain way.

This is the real point. We ourselves are a part of the chaos or chance that is the universe at its Absolute level. But we are the same part of that chaos as the world that we perceive. The order that we see, or create, is the result, or the reflection, of the particular chaos that is contained in us.

Thus order is created from chaos. On a purely physical level, evolution is a matter of chance. The process begins with a set of chance events or mutations. From among these one is selected, then amplified. In this way there may result a novel structure at the macroscopic level. In the words of Chuang Tzu: 'The Universe and I came into being together, and I, and everything therein are One.'

The universe proceeds along the path of least resistance. Once change has been effected, it, too, continues on the basis of relative inaction which then provides a further development in the overall genetic make-up and DNA structure which can be seen in the principle of morphic resonance described by Rupert Sheldrake.[2]

We and the world 'out there' have created each other. Both came into being together and therefore both are one – and also two. Both are the result of chance, but both are the result of the same chance. Our chaos and the chaos that is our world is the same, and the order that we perceive in the chaos is the order that exists in both the outerworld and in ourselves.

This is why there is unity. This is why inner and outer inevitably reflect each other and why the universe as a whole is described in each moment and for all time in its parts, in the motions of the planets and the flight of the birds, in the events that happen to us throughout our lives and in the people we continually attract.

And this, too, is why there is division. For we can only see by way of reflection. Consciousness means that we reflect and we need something upon which to reflect. On one level we, like the universe, simply are. When we are in this state of wholeness then we are aware of the quality of the universe around us. Then we do not need Astrology to point the way, we no longer need to learn by events. Then we just know.

When we are in our normal human state, we need the division that is implied in consciousness. We need to act as well as to be. We need to experience the duality that makes up our life on Earth. Then we can get more nearly towards a state of unity by understanding the principles and events that are reflected in the planetary motions.

In this way we can resolve the parts with the whole and learn to live in accordance with both our material and our spiritual nature. Every part of the space-time continuum has its own peculiar, individual characteristic and quality. Each separate part, the planets, Signs, Houses and aspects, are imbued with their own meaning, their archetypal significance.

If we look to see what is actually happening when the planets move in their orbits, we see that a particular area of the space-time continuum is being disturbed according to the value of a specific vibration, and that vibration will affect any other part of the universe, depending on the innate pattern of vibration that was formed at the time of its birth.

No two patterns which are described at any time will be the same for the relationship between the constituent parts will always be different, and this applies equally to the pattern that is formed at birth and the subsequent pattern that resonates in the universe as it harmonizes with the Horoscope.

Hence each one of us is unique and each of us has his or her own path to follow in accordance with the star under which we were born which is our personal Horoscope. Equally each one of us is a part of the whole for we are all brought into being as a part of the same universe, created by and as an element of the same divine order.

2 GOD'S MIRROR – A MYTH FOR MODERN MAN

In ascent or descent there is no fixed rule, except that one must do nothing evil. In advance or retreat no sustained perseverance avails, except that one must not depart from one's nature. The superior man fosters his character and labours at his task in order to do everything at the right time. Therefore he makes no mistake.

CONFUCIUS

In *Mysterium Coniunctionis* Jung recounts the story of a rainmaker. In a province of China there was a great drought. In desperation the local people called a rainmaker from another part of the land. When he arrived, the rainmaker locked himself up in a little hut for three days and then, on the fourth day, the rains came.

When the rainmaker was asked how he had produced this miracle, he denied responsibility. 'But what have you done these three days?' he was asked. 'Oh, I can explain that. I come from another country where things are in order. Here they are out of order, they are not as they should be by the ordinance of heaven. Therefore the whole country is not in Tao, and I also am not in the natural order of things because I am in a disordered country. So I had to wait three days until I was back in Tao and then naturally the rain came.'[3]

This parable aptly illustrates both the need to be in accord with our own nature and the connection between inner and outer. The message is clear. In order to put the world in order, we need first to put ourselves in order, and this means living up to the whole of our being, to the Self which in its completeness is symbolized by the Horoscope.

We have looked out into the world. We have looked into the sky, at the planets moving through space and time. We have observed the correlation between those heavenly bodies and our own lives. We have asked: 'How?' and 'Why?'

The time of questioning is almost over. Now it is time to experience the answers, to make them a part of ourselves. And to recognize how closely the answers depend on the questions themselves. We ask the purpose of Astrology. It is to help people to understand themselves and the universe of which they are a part.

We ask the meaning of Astrology. It is to realize the connection of inner and outer. And by 'realize' I mean experience in the sense of making real. 'The needful thing is not to "know" the truth,' said Jung, 'but to EXPERIENCE it.' We can ask why there is a correlation between the heavenly bodies and events on Earth, and answer that at its highest level the universe is a whole.

We can both experience it as a whole and we can also see it in its constituent parts, for the whole is reflected in each part. It is the understanding, or the realization, of the connection between the separate parts – the moment of time, the orbit of

Mars, the birth of an individual or event – with the whole, that provides the meaning of Astrology.

The philosopher will ask: 'Why?' To provide the meaning, the myth for man in this Age, we need to be in touch with ourselves and with the universe. This is what Astrology provides in its essence.

No amount of intellectual rationalization can bring us nearer to this truth. 'I believe in order to understand,' said Anselm. We can see that our lives on Earth are reflected in the movements of the planets and indeed by everything else around us.

It is perfectly valid to seek the explanation for this connection; it is perfectly natural to ask why it should be so. We have been created in order to question ever since the serpent of wisdom first tempted Eve to taste of the Tree of Knowledge. But asking questions is not enough.

If we simply ask questions we shall be in danger of missing the most obvious truth by the very blindness of our knowledge. Adam and Eve could have eaten of the Tree of Life which stood in the very centre of the garden. All they had to do was to stretch out their hands and eat and live for ever. God had not forbidden them to taste of this Tree. He simply placed it in front of them where they could not possibly miss it, and thereby ensured that they did not see it.

In asking 'why' and 'how' we can miss the vitally important fact that there is a correlation between the heavenly bodies and ourselves. We can be so busy working out what this correlation is, that we fail to experience it. The universe is described in its parts. Everything that happens 'out there' is a part of the whole, and if its meaning is recognized, it should bring us nearer to the whole.

The meaning is contained in the union of inner and outer, in the realization that they are the same. In bringing the two together, so that we and the universe become a living process. The danger lies in doing precisely the opposite and separating inner from outer. We can either recognize that we and the bodies in the sky are integral parts of one system. Or we can just see the planets 'out there' and regard them as alien forces.

That this is both a vital need and an increasng danger for mankind today should be clear. This is a time when we are free to choose our future as we reach the intersection between two Great Ages. Some have looked towards this time with fear and trepidation. The very year this book is being written, 1984, has been engraved on our minds by George Orwell's horrifying presentiment of the future.

Even the scientists have been filled with foreboding. In 1970 a group of them gathered at the Ames Research Centre of NASA to discuss the possibility of extraterrestrial intelligent life and the chances of communicating with such creatures.

On the basis of the number of stars in the universe it was decided that the rate at which other technical communities, which could contact each other, were likely to be formed would be approximately one in every ten years.

In these circumstances it would appear that there should be many millions of similar communities in the universe. But that optimistic assessment was subject to one fatal proviso. By the time that such intelligent forms of life had reached the stage of being able to communicate, the likely time of their survival would be drastically reduced. The time suggested by the Ames group was just ten years – the same as the rate at which such communities are being formed.

Others have eagerly awaited the Aquarian Age as a time of fulfilment and new hope; a time of understanding, when humanity can at last come into its own. There is no doubt that this is the most critical time that we have so far seen in the history of the world.

I believe that mankind has now reached a new stage in its evolution when we will be able to use our powers to widen our understanding as never before. Whether we use these powers to help humanity and the rest of life or to destroy it depends on the realization of our role and place in the universe.

What we need to do in order to provide mankind with the meaning it seeks, is to bring about the unity of the individual with the whole. The way to achieve this is a paradox. For as the story of the rainmaker showed, in order to provide harmony in the world, we need to establish harmony within ourselves.

Astrology enables us to do this because in the symbolism of the Horoscope we can see, and experience, the Self that we need to become. The paradox is that the Horoscope is the moment we are born, and as such it is the pattern that exists at that moment and at no other.

Once that moment has passed, the universe will never again be the same. It may therefore be thought that to align ourselves with the universe as it is at a particular time, we should function in accordance with that time rather than with the time of our birth.

That, however, is not so. For in separating our actions from our selves, we alienate ourselves both from our true nature and from the universe. This is indeed what has happened in our civilization. We are no longer a part of ourselves. In separating inner from outer, we have alienated ourselves from our source and from each other.

The situation appears to be a paradox because we are aligning our personal Horoscope with the ever changing pattern in the universe at any particular time, indeed at all times. In other words, we are combining Kronos with Kairos. The paradox is resolved when we recognize that we are a part of the whole, and that the moment we are born is not only a separate moment of time, but it is a part of the whole, and like any other part, the whole is reflected in it.

This, as I have stressed, means learning to see in a new way, in a way which I have called the fifth dimension. Then we see the individuality, the uniqueness of our lives which implies separation, together with the unity of all life. The ability to see in this way, to experience ourselves in the fifth dimension, is the contribution that Astrology has to offer mankind as we enter the Aquarian Age.

Individuality and separateness imply time and change. Union implies eternity and containment. The former is embodied in the latter, as we can see in the symbol of the Tao – the circle containing the opposites of yang and yin, which themselves include the essence of each other. As Heraclitus said: 'Good and evil are one. God is day and night, summer and winter, war and peace, surfeit and hunger.'

When we live up to the individuality which is symbolized in the Horoscope, then we are a part of the change that exists in time. And when we live up to that individuality in its wholeness that is the Self, then we are a part of the unity that is the universe. Then time and eternity become aspects of a living process.

Then by being we become. That is why it took three days for the rains to come. The rainmaker had to be at one with himself, at one with all time. Then, the general stream of time coincided, on the fourth day, with his moment of time. Then the rain came. Then, at the right time, came the intersection of the timeless with time.

So what do we do to align inner with outer – to be in Tao? It is easy to think that we do nothing. To look at the rainmaker and perceive no action on his part. To deride the man who prays instead of taking up his sword and fighting for peace. But the rainmaker produced the rain. He united Heaven with Earth and reconciled the two.

In a sense he did nothing. There is nothing to do except to be ourselves. Søren Kierkegaard has said that the purpose of life is 'to be the self which one truly is.' And Montaigne that 'the greatest thing in the world is to know how to belong to ourselves.'[4] If we are aligned with our true selves, then, when the time is right, union will take place. This is what happens in prayer. We get in touch with the whole by aligning our pattern with itself; at some time in the future, our prayers are answered. This is what happens in psychology – we accept the opposing parts of our nature, the separateness, we endure the tension. Then, when the time is right, the healing process takes place.

Yun-Men was asked: 'What is the Tao?' He replied: 'Walk on.' The Tao is the way. We can only walk upon it. But we also are the way. Jesus said: 'I am the way, the truth, and the life.'[5] We each have our own way. Our actions consist in walking upon it and experiencing it. 'In whatever way a human being shall seek me,' said Krishna to Arjuna, 'in that way can he find me. The paths are many, but ultimately, all come to me.'

We may think it is easy to just keep on walking. But the temptations to stray, to walk upon another's path, are many. We can see how difficult it is when we think how few there are who are at peace with themselves and with the world. We can see the difference in those who are battered by every passing transit which tries to blow the alienated individual back upon his course, and those who dance in motion with the planets, executing a timeless rhythm in accordance with the harmony of the spheres.

The magician, as archetypal man, as number 1 in the Tarot arcana, does nothing. He stands between Heaven and Earth. He is. The astrologer as magician, as archetypal man, Adam Kadmon, seeks to be himself, all that is contained within the wheel of his Horoscope.

The world is our world. As Seneca put it: 'Within the world there can be no exile, for nothing within the world is alien to man.' This world is contained in the circle of the Horoscope. What matters is how we view it. At the beginning of our journey it is 0, the Fool. It beckons us on full of promise and hope. We step over the precipice in our innocence and faith, knowing that God will uphold us.

Half way through our journey, as the 10, it is the Wheel of Fortune. Then we are bound to our material existence, we are like Ixion, on the outside, unable to get off. Things happen to us. We are cut off from the centre.

At the end of our journey we meet the wheel again. The last card is the Universe. Here we are in the world, at the centre, free, integrated with our source. Now it is our world and we are united in our love, with it.

When we are in touch with ourselves, when we experience ourselves, then we are in harmony. Then we know and love ourselves. And in the words of Clement of Alexandria: 'He who knows himself knows God.' Then we establish the correlation between ourselves and the rest of the universe. Then, when the time is right, the universe will respond.

Then, like the rainmaker, we will be aligned with our inner nature. Then we will not destroy the universe, nor the life that God has granted us. Then we shall live, and live in every moment. Then we shall appreciate the meaning of time and realize that if we truly live and experience each moment of time, we shall live eternally, for each moment will be for us, eternity.

There is harmony in the world on both the physical and the spiritual levels. We create harmony in the physical world by our senses, by the way we choose and discriminate. And we create harmony in the spiritual world by living in accordance with our Horoscopes.

We create the Divine Order in the universe, the divinity which is reflected in us when we are truly in touch with our spiritual natures, with God and the Christ within us. Then outer and inner reflect each other and the marriage of Heaven and Earth is consummated.

In this way we experience the myth that is contained in the Horoscope. Instead of using Astrology, we will have learned to live it. And by learning to live it, we shall help mankind to take the next step that we are poised to take in our evolution. Then a living Astrology, which links the spiritual and the human, will lead us into a new age.

> To communicate with Mars, converse with spirits...
> Describe the horoscope, haruspicate or scry,
> Observe disease in signatures, evoke
> Biography from the wrinkles of the palm
> And tragedy from fingers... all these are usual
> Pastimes and drugs... But to apprehend
> The point of intersection of the timeless
> With time, is an occupation for the saint....
> For most of us, there is only the unattended
> Moment, the moment in and out of time,
> The distraction fit, lost in a shaft of sunlight,
> The wilde thyme unseen, or the winter lightning
> Or the waterfall, or music heard so deeply
> That it is not heard at all, but you are the music
> While the music lasts.
>
> T.S. ELIOT, 'The Dry Salvages'

Notes

1 WHAT IS TRUTH? – A SEARCH FOR MEANING

1 Translated and reproduced by the *Astrological Journal*, June 1962, from R. Tomaschek, *Tradition und Fortschritt der Klassischen Astrologie*.
2 C.G. Jung, *Memories, Dreams, Reflections*, London, Collins, 1963, p. 237.
3 B. Russell, *The Problems of Philosophy*, Oxford, Oxford University Press, 1982, p. 71.
4 Russell, op. cit., p. 93.

2 THE NATURE OF PHYSICAL REALITY

1 Michel Gauguelin holds a degree in psychology and statistics and has carried out a considerable amount of research into the correlation between the planetary cycles and life on earth. He has written, *inter alia*, *The Cosmic Clocks* and *Astrology and Science*. Geoffrey Dean is an analytical chemist, science writer and astrologer and has compiled *Recent Advances in Natal Astrology*.
2 R. Jones, *Physics as Metaphor*, London, Abacus, 1983, p. 215.
3 B. Russell, *The Problems of Philosophy*, Oxford, Oxford University Press, 1982, p. 11.
4 Jones, op. cit., p. 207.
5 Quoted in M. Capek, *The Philosophical Impact of Contemporary Physics*, Princeton, D. Van Nostrand, 1961, p. 7.
6 Quoted in L. Cooper, *An Introduction to the Meaning and Structure of Physics*, New York, Harper & Row, 1968, p. 431.
7 J. Lindsay, *Origins of Astrology*, London, Frederick Muller, 1971, p. 420.
8 Quoted in Capek, op. cit., p. 319.
9 N. Calder, *Einstein's Universe*, Harmondsworth, Penguin Books, 1982, p. 212.
10 W. Heisenberg, *On Modern Physics*, New York, Clarkson Potter, 1961, p. 13.

11 H.P. Stapp, 'S-Matrix Interpretation of Quantum Theory', *Physical Review*, vol. D3 (15 March 1971), p. 1310.
12 Quoted in M. Gardner, *The Ambidextrous Universe*, Harmondsworth, Penguin Books, 1982, p. 204.
13 Article in *Nature*, vol. 310, 12 July 1984.
14 Quoted in Talbot, op. cit., p. 27.
15 P. Davies, *Other Worlds*, London, J.M. Dent & Son, 1980, p. 68.
16 R. Sheldrake, *A New Science of Life*, London, Granada, 1981, p. 114.
17 D. Bohm and B. Hiley, 'On the Intuitive Understanding of Nonlocality as Implied by Quantum Theory', *Foundations of Physics*, vol. 5 (1975).

3 HEAVEN AND EARTH – THE WORLD OF THE MAGICIAN

1 Matthew 18.20.
2 John 14.9.
3 M. Eckhart, *Sermons & Treatises*, vol. I, London, Watkins, 1979, p. 197.
4 I should make it clear that the use of biblical quotations throughout this book does not imply belief in the Christian, as opposed to any other, creed, but rather a closer acquaintance with the Bible.
5 Genesis 2.9.
6 Genesis 3.22.
7 D. Conway, *Magic An Occult Primer*, London, Jonathan Cape, 1972, p. 42.
8 M. Eckhart, op. cit., p. 121.
9 John 3.13.
10 John 7.34.
11 D. Fortune, *The Mystical Qabalah*, London, Ernest Benn, 1972, p. 17.
12 John 1.1.
13 M. Planck, *The Philosophy of Physics*, New York, Norton, 1936, p. 83.
14 I. Regardie, *Foundations of Practical Magic*, Wellingborough, The Aquarian Press, 1979, p. 29.
15 R. Jones, *Physics as Metaphor*, London, Abacus, 1983, p. 213.
16 G. Knight, *Experience of the Inner Worlds*, Cheltenham, Helios, 1975, p. 9.
17 D. Fortune, *Aspects of Occultism*, Wellingborough, The Aquarian Press, 1962, p. 17.
18 I Corinthians 13.11.

19 E.C. Whitmont, *The Symbolic Quest*, Princeton, Princeton University Press, 1969, p. 135.
20 Fortune, *The Mystical Qabalah*, op. cit., p. 287.
21 Ibid., p. 106.

4 THE MYSTERY OF TIME

1 M. Shallis, *On Time*, London, Burnett Books, 1982, p. 193.
2 In P.A. Schilpp (ed.), *Albert Einstein: Philosopher–Scientist*, Evanston, The Library of Living Philosophers, 1949, p. 250.
3 M. Eckhart, *Sermons & Treatises*, vol. I, London, Watkins, 1979, p. 163.
4 Ibid., p. 183.
5 Shallis, op. cit., p. 192.
6 E.C. Whitmont, *The Symbolic Quest*, Princeton, Princeton University Press, 1969, p. 78.
7 Eckhart, op. cit., p. 74.
8 Ecclesiastes 3. 14-15.
9 Revelations 21.4.
10 Quoted in A. Storr, *The Dynamics of Creation*, Harmondsworth, Pelican Books, 1976, p.294.
11 Shallis, op. cit., p. 81.
12 J.S. Bolen, *The Tao of Psychology*, London, Wildwood House, 1980, p. 48.
13 I am here combining the astral and higher mental levels into one for convenience.
14 Eckhart, op. cit., p.49.
15 Bolen, op. cit., p. 36.
16 Ecclesiastes 3.1-8.
17 Matthew 26.18.
18 Quoted in J. Lindsay, *Origins of Astrology*, London, Frederick Muller, 1971, pp. 158-9.

5 A VIEW OF THE FUTURE – PREDICTION AND FREE WILL

1 This is a hypothetical figure to illustrate the principle.
2 Matthew 11.25.
3 I. Regardie, *Foundations of Practical Magic*, Wellingborough, The Aquarian Press, 1979, p. 49.
4 Mark 13.31-2.
5 Acts 1.7.
6 F. Kafka, *The Trial*, London, Pan Books, 1977, pp. 239-40.

7 C.R. Rogers, *On Becoming a Person*, London, Constable, 1967, p. 157.
8 E.C. Whitmont, *The Symbolic Quest*, Princeton, Princeton University Press, 1969, p. 72.
9 Ibid., p. 91.
10 A. Storr, *The Integrity of the Personality*, Harmondsworth, Penguin Books, 1963, p. 170.
11 C.G. Jung, *Collected Works*, vol. 9, London, Routledge & Kegan Paul, 1978, pp. 70-1.
12 Matthew 11.29-30.
13 Whitmont, op. cit., p. 264.
14 I use the term 'directions' here to include all predictive techniques.

6 THE FIRMAMENT – REALITY AND PERCEPTION

1 G. Zukav, *The Dancing Wu Li Masters*, London, Fontana/Collins, 1979, p. 115.
2 The 'super-hologram of reality' is a concept put forward by Charles Muses and Arthur M. Young in *Consciousness and Reality*, New York, Outerbridge & Lazard, 1972.
3 E.C. Whitmont, *The Symbolic Quest*, Princeton, Princeton University Press, 1969, p. 28.

7 JACOB'S LADDER

1 C.G. Jung, *Modern Man in Search of a Soul*, New York, Harcourt, Brace & Co., 1933, p. 6.
2 Whitmont, op. cit., p. 51.
3 C.G. Jung, *Archetypes and the Collective Unconscious*, London, Routledge & Kegan Paul, 1959, par. 521.
4 Whitmont, op. cit., p. 310.
5 Ibid., p. 96.
6 A. Storr, *The Integrity of the Personality*, Harmondsworth, Penguin Books, 1963, p. 136.
7 C.G. Jung, *Memories, Dreams, Reflections*, London, Collins, 1963, p. 196.
8 Storr, op. cit., p. 136.
9 C.R. Rogers, *On Becoming a Person*, London, Constable, 1967, p. 175.

10 Storr, op. cit., p. 27.

8 THE FIFTH DIMENSION

1 F. Capra, *The Tao of Physics*, London, Fontana/Collins, 1975, p. 195.
2 D. Bohm and B. Hiley, 'On the Intuitive Understanding of Nonlocality as Implied by Quantum Theory', *Foundations of Physics*, vol. 5 (1975).
3 J.S. Bolen, *The Tao of Psychology*, London, Wildwood House, 1980, p. 41.
4 C.G. Jung, *Memories, Dreams, Reflections*, London, Collins, 1963, p. 325.
5 Quoted in F.C. Happold, *Religious Faith & Twentieth-Century Man*, London, Darton, Longman and Todd, 1980, p. 179.

9 NUMBER – THE PATTERN BEHIND REALITY

1 The frequency is the number of crests passing a stationary observer in a second; the wavelength is the distance between the adjacent crests; the speed is the wavelength (λ) x the frequency (f).
2 The frequency of visible light is about five million billion vibrations a second.
3 F. Capra, *The Tao of Physics*, London, Fontana/Collins, 1975, p. 261.
4 M. Eckhart, *Sermons & Treatises*, vol. I, London, Watkins, 1979, p. 95.
5 M. Buber, *I and Thou*, transl. R.G. Smith, Edinburgh, T & T Clark, 1953, p. 28.
6 In secondary progressions, one day is equal to one year, while in the 'one-degree' method one degree is equal to one year. One degree is the approximate area of the ecliptic travelled by the Sun in one day.
7 Quoted in G. Adler, *Studies in Analytical Psychology*, New York, C.G. Jung Foundation, 1966, pp. 120-1.

10 THE UNION OF HEAVEN AND EARTH

1 Quoted in H. Blamires, *A Short History of English Literature*, London, Methuen & Co., 1974, pp. 98-9.

2 This concept is put forward by R. Sheldrake in *A New Science of Life*, London, Granada, 1981.
3 C.G. Jung, *Mysterium Coniunctionis*, London, Routledge & Kegan Paul, 1965, p. 419.
4 *The Essays of Montaigne*, transl. E.J. Trechmann, The Modern Library Edition, 1946, p. 206.
5 John 14.6.

Index

Adams, John Couch, 71
Addey, John, 14
Akashic records, 36, 85, 87
Anki, 12, 61, 116, 136
Apollo, 134
archetypes, 113-14, 123, 127
Aristotle, 22
Assiah, 37, 41, 47, 155
astral: body, 47; level, 36, 68, 87, 135, 143-4, 157, 171; plane, 38, 40, 47, 50, 68; world, 35
Atziluth, 37, 41, 47-8, 148
Augustine, Saint, 118
Aurelius, Marcus, 91

Bell's theorem, 143
Binah, 44, 66
black hole, 144
Blake, William, 107-9, 112
Blyth, R.H., 110
Bohm, David, 31, 142
Bohr, N., 25, 34, 36, 155
Bolen, Jean, 67-8, 147
Briah, 37, 41
Broglie, Louis de, 57
Browning, Robert, 13, 64
Brummer-Trant, Emma, 60
Buber, Martin, 161
Buddha, 71, 172
Burr, Harold Saxton, 35

Calder, Nigel, 23
Capra, F., 138, 145, 156
Carroll, Lewis, 111
causation, 6, 30, 66, 69, 136, 145-6, 151
chakras, 139-40, 167
Chardin, Teilhard de, 11, 151
Chase, C.T., 71

Chesed, 44, 53
Chladni figures, 158
Chokmah, 44, 66
Chuang-Tzu, 110, 174
Clement of Alexandria, 181
Confucius, 71, 118-19, 175
conservation of parity, 16, 23, 26, 71
Conway, David, 40, 44

Daath, 44
Davies, Paul, 31
Dean, Geoffrey, 15
dekans, 76, 79
Dike, 74
dimension *see* fifth dimension
directions, 104, 165-7
divination, 87-8
double-slit experiment, 24, 145

Eckhart, Meister, 13, 39, 42, 60-1, 68, 110, 160
ecliptic, 56, 63
Ego, the, 126-8
Einstein, Albert, 20-4, 29-30, 55, 139, 144; Einstein–Rosen–Podolsky paradox, 30, 69, 82, 143, 145; field theory, 21, 29; relativity theory, 21, 30, 143
Eirene, 74
Eliot, T.S., 6, 12, 14-15, 59-60, 84-5, 89, 95, 101, 113, 115, 125, 182
Emerson, 94, 129
Enlil, 12, 62
eternity, 12-13
etheric: body, 35-6, 38, 47; plane, 50; world, 35
Eunomia, 74

INDEX

Feynman, 84
Fides, 8
fifth dimension, 135-53, 179
Fortune, Dion, 46, 50, 52-3
Frankl, Victor, 100
freedom, and free will, 81, 84-106, 157; freedom of matter, 155
frequency, 156, 158, 166
Freud, Sigmund, 130
Fu-Chih, Wang, 155

Gaia, 61, 120
Gauguelin, Michel, 15, 83
Geburah, 44, 53, 113
Gibbs, Willard, 29
god forms, 8-9

Hegel, 142
Heisenberg, Werner, 24-5, 31, 156-7
Heraclitus, 124, 170, 179
Hike, 46
Hitler, 47, 71
holographic theory, 142
Horai, 74
horary astrology, 5

Iamblichus, 48
I Ching, 68, 71, 103
intuition, 2, 116-17; intuitive faculties, 14, 49, 109, 121

Jeans, Sir James, 28
Jenny, Hans, 158
John XXIII, Pope, 75
Jones, Roger, 18
Jung, Carl G., 6, 47, 51, 64, 66, 91, 93-4, 97, 101, 108, 114, 118, 121, 123, 127, 130-1, 137, 146, 175-6

kabbalah, 39-40, 45, 52-3, 93, 114, 131, 167
Kafka, Franz, 90
Kairos, 59, 75, 79, 179
Kay, Norman, 64
Keats, John, 35
Kepler, 154
Kether, 42, 46, 136-7, 161
Kierkegaard, Søren, 180
Knight, Gareth, 49

Kronos, 59, 61-2, 64, 75, 79, 179

Laplace, Pierre, 19, 24, 82
Lee, Tsung Dao, 26
lepton, 28
level: of existence, 37, 48, 68; of reality, 1, 135; sub-atomic, 24-5, 29, 35, 50, 58, 82-3, 88, 141, 143-4, 157
Leverrier, Urbaine, 71
L-fields, 35
light: paradox of, 144, 161; speed of, 21-2, 30, 143, 145
Lindsay, Jack, 20
Lovelace, Richard, 96

magic, 19, 39, 40, 48-9, 53, 158; magician, 1-2, 15, 19, 34-5, 39, 45-7, 50, 52, 161, 181
Malkuth, 44, 136-7, 172
Manilius, Marcus, 139
matrix mechanics, 32; theory of, 156
Michelson, A.A., 20
mind, 1, 34, 36, 46, 49, 107-17, 119, 139, 142; the Higher Mind, 38, 79, 87, 135
Mithra, religion of, 63, 167-8
Montaigne, 180
Moon, changing colour of, 7; physical effects of, 6
morphic resonance, 31
mystic, 1, 3, 17, 51, 59-61, 63, 124, 151, 154

Nasatya, 63
Nemesis, 74, 93
Netzach, 44
Newton, Isaac, 21, 23, 55, 71, 154
numbers: meaning of, 41-5, 66, 78, 154-69; quantum, *see* quantum numbers; whole, 24

Ouranos, 61, 120

Paracelsus, 123
Pasteur, Louis, 26
Pauli, Wolfgang, 26-7
perception, 107-10
Planck, Max, 47

INDEX

planetary orbits, 162-9
Plato, 66
Plotinus, 92
Popper, Karl, 33
prediction, 39, 80-106; scientific, 26
Pribram, Karl, 142
psyche, 3, 118, 121-9, 152
psychology, 48, 51, 114, 118, 120-9
Ptolemy, 22
Pythagoras, 154, 158

quantum: interconnectedness, 31; level, *see* sub-atomic level; numbers, 49, 156; physics, 57; revolution, 16, 23, 82, 155; theory, 22-6, 28, 30
quark, 28

rational: explanation, 14; faculty, 2, 49; function, 10, 109
Regardie, Israel, 48, 88
Rogers, Carl, 91, 95, 128
Rousseau, Jean-Jacques, 80
Russell, Bertrand, 9-11, 13, 18, 22, 58, 85, 136, 158, 160-1; law of identity, 11, 136, 161

Salus, 8
Schopenhauer, 96
Self, the, 126-34, 176, 178-9
Seneca, 93, 183
sephira, sephiroth, 41, 45, 53, 160
Shakespeare, 71, 81
Shallis, Michael, 54, 60
Sheldrake, Rupert, 31, 174
Sidney, Sir Philip, 170
Socrates, 9-10, 13
space/time continuum, 56-7, 104, 138, 149-50, 162, 164-6, 168
spiritual: dimension, 10; laws, 93; level, 1, 11, 59, 68, 86-8, 100, 108, 135-6, 148, 150-1, 154, 157; world, 13, 35, 38, 55
Stapp, Henry, 25
statistics, 83-4, 103, 116
Stobaios, 76
Storr, Anthony, 93, 126, 128-9
sub-atomic, *see* level
symbolism, 14, 123, 130, 151, 158, 178; symbols, 32, 39, 49-50, 52, 113-17, 130
symmetry, 20, 26-7, 84
synchronicity, 6, 30, 66-9, 136, 145-6, 151

T'an Ching, 68
tarot, 14, 20, 42, 45, 52, 87, 103, 114, 131, 181
telesmatic images, 48
Tellus, 8
Teresa, Mother, 96
Thales, 71
Thoth, 46
time, 12, 21, 54-79, 84, 149, 179; of birth, 5; cycles of, 70-2, 149; moment of, 2-3, 13, 64, 71, 75, 78-9, 104, 146, 149, 164, 176; mythological, 60; qualities of, 70; unity of, 86; *see also* space/time continuum
Tiphareth, 44
Tomaschek, Rudolf, 3
transit, 52, 165-7
Tree of Life, 40, 44, 52, 97-8, 127, 131, 136, 139, 160-1, 167, 177
Twain, Mark, 18

Vestal Virgins, 9
vibration, rate of, 156-8, 165, 168

Whitmont, Edward, 92-3, 100, 113, 122, 125
Wiener, Norbert, 29
Wilson, Colin, 67
Wirth, Oswald, 52
Wu, Chien-Shiung, 26, 71

Yang, Chen Ning, 26
Yesod, 44
Yetzirah, 37, 41, 155
Yun-Men, 180

Zervan Akarana, 63
Zodiac, 7, 56, 61, 75, 77, 79; Signs of the, 8, 48, 76-7, 112, 164, 175
Zohar, 62
Zoroaster, 71
Zukav, Gary, 109